Chakras
& Shadow
Work

About the Author

Stefani Michelle is an interfaith minister, reiki master, yoga instructor, and cognitive coach. Stefani holds master's degrees in education and leadership, and she is the founder of Primal Heart Healing, through which she offers life coaching and intuitive healing. She has been working with clients for more than twenty years. Visit her on Facebook at facebook.com/primalhearthealing/.

Chakras
& Shadow
Work

Align Your Energy
Centers and Explore
Your Hidden Self

STEFANI MICHELLE

Llewellyn Publications
Woodbury, Minnesota

FIRST EDITION
First Printing, 2024

Cover design by Verlynda Pinckney
Interior art by the Llewellyn Art Department

Llewellyn Publications is a registered trademark of Llewellyn Worldwide Ltd.

Library of Congress Cataloging-in-Publication Data (Pending)
ISBN: 978-0-7387-7745-0

Llewellyn Worldwide Ltd. does not participate in, endorse, or have any authority
or responsibility concerning private business transactions between our authors
and the public.

All mail addressed to the author is forwarded but the publisher cannot, unless
specifically instructed by the author, give out an address or phone number.

Any internet references contained in this work are current at publication time,
but the publisher cannot guarantee that a specific location will continue to be
maintained. Please refer to the publisher's website for links to authors' websites
and other sources.

Llewellyn Publications
A Division of Llewellyn Worldwide Ltd.
2143 Wooddale Drive
Woodbury, MN 55125-2989
www.llewellyn.com

Printed in the United States of America

Dedication

This book is dedicated to my mother. She knew when I was very young that I was different. It wasn't easy for her to raise such a wild, vivid mind, but she never gave up. She became a metaphysical master just to understand and nurture my mind. I gave her lots of sleepless nights while I navigated through time and space, but she persevered even when I pretended to be normal like the other kids. She never stopped supporting me and teaching me and encouraging me to find my way. Everything I know and everything I am is because of her.

Disclaimer

The material in this book is not intended as a substitute for trained medical or psychological advice. Readers are advised to consult their personal healthcare providers regarding treatment. If experiencing a mental health crisis, please contact a licensed professional. The publisher and the author assume no liability for any injuries caused to the reader that may result from the reader's use of the content contained herein and recommend common sense when contemplating the practices described in the work.

Other Books by Stefani Michelle

The Beast

Put light against light—you have nothing.
Put dark against dark—you have nothing.
It's the contrast of light and dark
that each gives the other one meaning.
~ *Bob Ross*

Contents

Introduction

Chakras and Shadow Work will enable you to strengthen, empower, and purge your energy. It will help you create a flow that will accelerate your vibration by learning how to clear your physical and emotional energy bodies, open and expand your spiritual and wisdom energy bodies, and connect to your bliss body.

Chakras and Shadow Work teaches you how to create a flow of energy throughout your entire bodies that will enhance your life and magical abilities. You will learn what elements and tools connect to each chakra to enhance the vibration. You will learn how to connect with and love your shadow self through meditations that align to each chakra energy center as well as how to utilize the psychic abilities that stem from each chakra and how best to practice and enhance each ability. You will also learn yoga sequences that unblock each chakra as well as tea recipes for each. This book is full of tricks and tools to create a magical life, from incense to questions you'll ask yourself. The meditations, rituals, yoga sequences, gemstones, oils and herbs, and psychic practices provided will help you align to your higher self and the best version of your life.

Chakras and Shadow Work is broken down by chakras, which are seven main energy centers located along the spine, from the base to the crown. This book should be read in order the first time to create a foundation of healing and building. When doing shadow work, it is extremely beneficial to focus on each energy center, one at a time. Chakras hold memory like a clogged drain, and like water not flowing through a clogged drain, your energy cannot flow freely through a clogged chakra. Chakras become clogged when we experience trauma that alters our natural state of being; shadow work allows us to reclaim our natural state of being. The alignment of emotion and stuck energy within each chakra is what gives us our flow through life. When we can clear the chakras and emotions, as well as characteristics of each, we can have a well-balanced and joyful life. You can always come back to any chapter and study one chakra at a time according to what energies you are working with in your own body. This book is designed to be used over and over again, year after year. You may want to keep a journal of your journey and look back at all the wonderful things that have manifested while working through this book.

Each chapter is broken down into seven main sections: Tools and Properties, Shadow Work, Tea Recipes, Movement and Yoga Sequence, Meditations, Rituals, and Psychic Center. I will first describe the chakra the chapter is about, then in Tools and Properties, I provide a list of emotional connections, physical connections, foods, activities, color, element, tones and notes, gemstones, and oils and herbs that work with and align each chakra.

In shadow work, I will provide prompts to ask yourself in order to find if that chakra is out of balance and where you have been using your own personal energy in destructive ways. You will be encouraged to bring up parts of your personality that you have hidden in the shadows and are ashamed of in order to heal that energy.

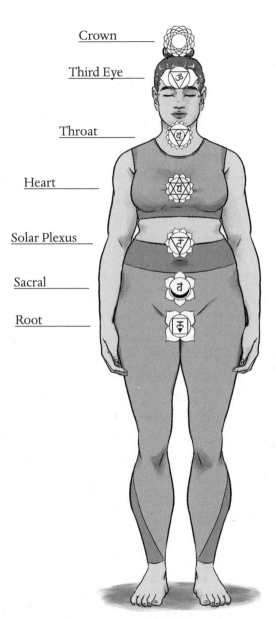

Crown

Third Eye

Throat

Heart

Solar Plexus

Sacral

Root

The Chakras

The section called Recipes features herbal tea blends that I have created and written incantations to go along with. I like to make and drink these teas with water that has been energized by the moon.

For Movement and Yoga Sequence, I will provide a short routine of yoga poses that will specifically open and align the chakra we are working with. If you are unfamiliar with yoga poses, you should consult an instructor to ensure you are getting into the poses safely and correctly. The meditations are guided visualizations that I feel work best when working with certain chakras; however, each one can be used for any chakra and personal practice. You may want to record yourself reading the guided visualization and then play it back with music when you are ready to practice it. If you have a hard time with visualization, you may want to focus on just the words.

The rituals that I will be providing are not your usual candle work or circlecasting. You may see some of that throughout the book; however, these rituals I provide are focused on energy movement in order to accomplish the changes in your life you desire. These are practices that will create a ripple effect of energy in your future days. You will begin to see the results of this energy work and how it is being manifested in your life. These are all rituals that I have had great success with.

Finally, the psychic center is an alignment to divination tools and how each chakra has an ability to work within the universal consciousness and predict patterns and outcomes as well as connect with the unseen.

A Little about Me

I grew up, as many of us do, with trauma that gave me terrible anxiety and even worse coping skills. I trusted no one in my life—

not family, nor friends. I created a story about my life that I now realize was nothing but perceived realities fueled by years of suffering. I brought my fears to life and lived them on repeat.

I have degrees in communications, education, and leadership. I am a certified interfaith minister, reiki master, yoga instructor, and cognitive coach. Each time I studied something new, I was chasing healing. I tried healing in a traditional way. I tried talk therapy a few times over the course of my life. I tried spirituality. It wasn't until I started asking myself the hard questions and facing the part of myself that I had denied that I started to find happiness in my life.

My life's mission became learning how to heal and teaching others what I've learned. *Chakras and Shadow Work* is about how to create a life of magic after recovery from codependency, narcissism, and psychic trauma. The good parts of my life became the tools I used, and over a lifetime of learning and teaching, I have picked up a lot of tools. I would say this book is an entire metaphysical journey.

Chakras and Shadow Work will teach you how to reclaim your natural spiritual gifts and life. I will share how I remembered who I truly am and how you can as well. This book is about moving through your own journey of healing and magic. There is no end to this book. It is ever growing, ever evolving, and in constant motion just like you and me. One day you will be able to look back at the first time you picked up this book and realize your life has drastically changed and continues to do so.

During this journey, you will ask yourself questions about who you have become due to your experiences and what is still shaping your vision of the world. Who were you before the world influenced you, conditioned you, told you what to believe and how to behave? You will start to remember yourself, your energy, and your power and start living a magical life. Learning is life's adventure, food and sex are life's luxuries, and love is life's purpose.

Living a Life of Magic

Why *Chakras and Shadow Work*? We hold our memories in our bodies. Working with our energy bodies and the systems aligned to each allows us to release old patterns of survival in order to create new patterns. The life-force energy that flows within us and around us is directly related to how we show up in this world. When we align our body, mind, and spirit, we can truly live the life we want. I break down this book by each chakra because many people are ready but don't know where to start. I found that breaking it down by the chakras allows you to have a map into otherwise-uncharted areas, and the best place to start with that is at the foundation, and then we will build from there.

In Tools and Properties, you will find physical as well as emotional attributes that each chakra (energy system) aligns to. You can think of this section as vibrational matches that help enhance or heal each. Just like fruits and vegetables grow with different vitamins and nutrients that help the body, so do herbs and crystals. All of these things are produced by the earth, and as they grow, they absorb different minerals and vitamins, creating endless possibilities for healing and growing. The Tools and Properties section gives you multiple ways to align your energy.

I give you the tools to align your energy before we dive into shadow work so that you may have support during the shadow work process if you need it. You may have heard this term before, and simply put, it is looking at the parts of yourself that you are ashamed of, that you hide from the world, that you deny about yourself. This is the work that I call your abuse of power. When you dive deep into looking at these parts of yourself, the real heal-ing and magic become possible.

Everything is energy, and energy is always moving. Sometimes it feels like it's moving backward, other times like a speeding bul-let, and everything in between. Our bodies are also always moving and are the only real vehicle we have for this planet. You will not only learn to change your life; you will also become more aware of how to take care of your physical and energy bodies.

I include tea recipes with incantations that align to the magic of the life-force energy we are working on at that moment. Our bod-ies are composed of more water than anything else, and because of this, I find that herbal teas are very effective in aligning the body.

The tea incantations create an even more activated body of water that holds the intention for change you wish to create. You may be aware of the studies on words and energy with plants and water. There is a video I watched during my years in education that shows the different effects of encouraging words and bullying words on two plants. One plant is given praise and affection and the other plant is given words of discouragement and judgment. Both are fed and watered and given the same amount of sunlight; however, because of the words that are spoken, one plant withers and dies and the other grows tall and thrives.[1] I'm sure you can guess which is which. This is how our mind works on our bodies and another example of how powerful our belief system is.

Movement is very important when trying to create magic in your life. My best manifestations and meditations come when I am either dancing or on the treadmill. For the purposes of this book, I am going to give you just a few yoga poses that help move

---

1. "Bully A Plant: Say No To Bullying," IKEA UAE, YouTube video, 2:17, April 30, 2018, https://www.youtube.com/watch?v=Yx6UgfQreYY.

energy along in each of the chakras. There are many studies out there now about the effects of stuck energy in the body and how it becomes a physical illness.[2]

Early on in my studies, I heard my teacher say, "The dis-ease in the body becomes our disease." Later, I noticed that phrase being used a lot between healing practitioners. When trauma happens—any event that causes you to get knocked off your center—you create a block of energy, like a bruise that never heals. These blocks can wreak havoc on your nervous system. They can be as small as not seeing the object right in front of you to as big as not seeing the situation for what it is. When we intentionally unblock these "hits" of trauma, we may experience memories that caused the block or we may not, but either way, the flow of energy is restored. When this is restored in your body, your potential for superhuman power turns on.

While movement is about restoring the flow of energy in your body, meditation is about quieting the noise to find peace. The meditations in this book are visual journeys intended to get you in touch with your higher self and your superhuman potential. These meditations have been passed down to me through my mother. She hosted and led weekly teachings at my house when I was growing up, and now I am passing them down to you. These are the meditations that I used in my childhood to enhance my psychic connections to all things seen and unseen.

Then we get to rituals, which are the activities that you can use to actively participate in the restructuring of your reality. I don't call them magical spells because for me they are active, and we participate with them through an extended amount of time. Spells

2. Bessel A. van der Kolk, *The Body Keeps the Score: Brain, Mind, and Body in the Healing of Trauma* (New York: Viking, 2014).

are done to create a ripple effect of energy that, once you have completed them, take on a life of their own. Rituals need your continued participation. Each one of these rituals that I am passing on to you I have personally used and designed and have had great success with.

Welcome

I am excited for you to read this book, as it is filled with so many ways for you to create the life of your dreams. Let's start by building a new foundation. I believe we should be enjoying this life and planet and all its abundant treasures—enjoying life on our terms. We all have our healing paths, and sometimes we have to choose us over everyone else just to keep going. Sometimes the path of least destruction is still destruction, and that path is still judged. We may never see the tornado that was on the other path had it been chosen, but fuck it; do what it takes to heal. Only you can decide that your life is worth it!

Over a lifetime of healing, grieving, and learning about myself, I made a discovery. Each time I released something from my past that had created fear and anxiety, I changed my memories along with it. Healing and releasing old trauma removed memories from my brain that it had kept on a loop. This allowed happy memories from those years to become present. It was like reliving my childhood with laughter and joy. It also allowed more survival skills that I had developed to come to light. This became the way I started to retrain my brain.

I am often asked how to find and heal those deep layers that are stopping the vibration of joy. My answer is always the same: you can't just jump right down to the core; you have to slowly chip away at the outer layers before the deepest parts of you can be revealed. It doesn't matter where you start, just start. The magic will start to happen right away. Your experiences will start to change and serve your healing and journey to joy.

Nothing will help you until *you* are truly ready to help you. At that time, once you know the change is possible and that magic is real, it will continue to show up over and over again. I realized during my journey that I never believed I would find happiness; therefore, I never found it. Once you believe—truly and actually believe, once you know—watch the world show up for you. I say this because so many times working with clients, they will say, "I am ready. I believe it is for me, and it's still not showing up." If you truly believed, then the last part of that sentence would not exist because there would be no time, no ending, no finish line. It would just be. You wouldn't question it or have any reason to say, "It's still not showing up for me." If you know something will show up in your life, you won't get frustrated with how long it takes to show up. You just have faith that it will rather than fear that it won't or that it isn't. We need to change it from a belief to a knowing. When you know it to be true, you will see it, and still there will be no end, just a new beginning of creating.

I needed to change, make the decision to understand the highs and lows I experience. I needed to believe and know life could be different. I basically had to tell myself to cut that shit out. I had to retrain my brain, and I had to do it every day. Once I really committed to healing, everything started to work: spirituality worked, yoga worked, Co-Dependents Anonymous worked, and therapy worked. I had started to hear the world differently, and I became open to healing.

In the 12-step program of Co-Dependents Anonymous (CoDA), they ask you to identify your character defects. This is an extremely helpful process for people. In this book, you will read about how these are not defects at all but simply an abuse of your own power.

You may have heard it said before, but your greatest strength is also your greatest weakness. During your shadow work in each chakra, you will be faced with questions that I suggest you really sit with; unravel what each one means to you. These questions are helpful at every stage of your life. You should revisit the Shadow Work sections of this book often.

Chapter One
Creating Magic

We attach ourselves to people, places, things, outcomes, and expectations. We are always giving away our power. We are giving our power to our attachments. The things that we put before us become our attachments, our identity, the boxes we define ourselves by, thus creating limitations. If you are a mom, there's an expectation of a role you have to live up to. You can replace the word *mom* with anything, and I'm sure you can then describe the agenda for that identity, limiting your flow of energy. We are losing faith in our own flow of energy. I am going to be explaining how we hold different attachments and limitations in our chakras throughout the book, connecting each energy center to a certain flow.

You can't skip the healing part of your journey. You can't just simply put into place an emotional disposition of happiness, joy, and abundance. You have to look at how you lost those feelings to begin with and replace each belief of survival you acquired with a new belief in thriving. For example, an abandonment fear must be recognized first, then determined how it got there, then retaught. You will need to not only believe you are connected; you need to feel the connection.

The stronger our emotions, the more powerful things are—good or bad. We must focus our emotions to believe we are already in the vibration of what we want. I explain this as the bat signal. What we are signaling out based on our deep emotions is what we will get in return. You can do all the affirmations in the world, but if you don't actually believe them, you are just reciting words and are not changing your bat signal—that silent radar that pulses out from your heart, the vibration of your true thoughts and emotions. You can say, "I am beautiful," but that's not enough. If you are not also feeling beautiful, you will not project beauty. We become free of our desires or cravings because we are already in a state of believing they are happening. In this state, we can let go and just be. This is where the magic actually begins.

When I have clients for psychic readings, they seek confirmation of the existence of an alternative reality, meaning what the outcome of their free will and choices might be. Sometimes I see the pain they may go through in the future when they operate in the current patterns or reality. I have the ability to see what the healed version of them can accomplish. I don't believe all things are destined to be. I do this work so that my clients can take control of their own reality. I believe we create patterns, and according to the pattern we are living, we will most certainly have predictable outcomes. If we can remove ourselves from the pattern, take a bird's-eye view, we will see new options. That is what I do for my clients and myself now. I look from the spirits' perspective, the higher realm, and I use the options to create new patterns.

Freeing ourselves from our attachments, deeply understanding that the only thing in existence is energy, allows us to choose joy every time. Money no longer equates to suffering and survival; it becomes tangible energy that as a race of humans we have decided to use as an exchange system. I offer you my personal energy, and you offer me a holding place for energy I can use in the future to acquire more energy elsewhere. This is the tangible that will create more joy; however, once realized, it is just a placeholder. We can create other ways to exchange energy. You will notice when you let go of fear—fear of not having enough, fear of struggle, fear of survival—you create room for joy, and from that space comes the flow of money easily. Joy seeks more joy.

What about when you don't know what your spark is? What if all you can hear are the voices of your experience, and your own voice is lost among the chaos? This is the process of healing and also the spiritual awakening we seek. This is where the shadow work lives. We attach because we seek connection. We seek connection because we have forgotten God. (I am using the word *God* in this book to represent any higher power, and I am using it as a place word for *higher being* and *energy life force*.) We have been taught to believe that God's energy is separate from ourselves. We have been taught that there are conditions to hearing and feeling God, but there aren't. We are God. We are life energy connected to all living things. We have been conditioned to disconnect from our own God voice and allow someone else to dictate to us what that God energy is. We have given over our power to structures, systems, boxes, and images. We have attached ourselves to belief systems and ideas of what it means to be human instead of feeling and listening to our own energy and following its natural instincts. This is the true connection we have lost.

In order to hear God again, to create our life the way we want, to open up to our own psychic abilities, we must stop layering suffering with stories. These stories are manifestations of stress and trauma, and the more you believe the "stories," the more you reinforce this energy. This is how we keep getting the same thing over and over again. Stress occurs when we want something to be different than what it is at the moment and we don't know how to make that shift. The story of what it "should be" is an attachment to an ideal and the greatest form of suffering.

Shadow work is fighting all the ugly conditioning. There is no one way to do this. It is messy and it is hard, but eventually all you have left is a pure stream of flowing energy that is in continuous movement. That is why for this book I will start at our foundation, the root chakra, where most of our beliefs and attachments were formed. The rest of our story simply reinforces them.

How long you work with each chakra varies depending on how much you have been holding in each energy system, but typically I would recommend working with each for thirty days then moving to the next. You can cycle through them as often or as little as you like.

Chapter Two
Root Chakra, Muladhara

Located between the tailbone and the sexual organs, this energy center is the foundation of our system. When balanced, it keeps us present and grounded. The root is how we connect to the earth and recycle our energy through the ground beneath our feet. The root is our foundation, and we can look at it from a couple perspectives. It's our balance, like the roots of a tree; when we are grounded, we feel balanced and present. It's where we create safety, security, and trust.

The roots are the first things to grow, so we can also connect our childhood years to this energy system. The foundational years can determine our growth and how we created our survival skills in life. How were our basic human needs met, and what patterns do we have now because of this? Just like the roots in any living organism, they must be strong to thrive. Just like other living organisms, we can do work to create a healthy root system emotionally, physically, and spiritually.

I Am

The root chakra is related to the concept of self-identity, self-preservation, and the foundational aspects of one's existence.

Therefore, "I am" is a fundamental expression that represents a sense of self, one's existence, and basic survival instincts.

It seems so simple that this energy runs through all living things. To find the great "I am," we don't look outward, such as in a church or temple; we look within. I am the observer of this moment. I am an observer of this energy. I am the observer of this person. I am a living and breathing force. I am constant. I am a projection of energy and thought. I am conscious. What if I said to you that it is a statement of freedom, a statement of permission? As in, I give myself permission to feel and observe the feelings that come up at any time. I have the freedom to move through myself safely. What if I said it is a statement of faith? If I have faith in the moment, then I am how I choose to show up energetically.

Tools and Properties of the Root for Alignment

Emotional connections: Grounding, support, safety, security, basic human needs, transmutation, pleasure, desires—sexual or others, Kundalini, creativity, life force, earth connections, and strength

Physical connections: Colon, womb, sexual organs, urethra, prostate, legs, feet, hips, eliminatory system, base of the body, endocrine glands, adrenal glands, joints, and skeletal system

Foods: Beets, red berries, radishes, peppers, kidney beans, root vegetables

Activities: Walking, jogging

Color: Red—The root responds to reds and balances when fed red foods.

Element: Earth—Standing barefoot on grass, sand, dirt, or any natural earth floor can be very calming. It cleanses and balances your energy when you put the soles of your feet on the ground.

Tones and notes: C, ooh, or hew—Listening to music, sounds, and frequencies that have these in them can break up blocks and clear out energy in the root. Sounds can be a very healing tool for anyone to use. Attend a sound healing class or listen to frequencies on any music app.

Gemstones

Gemstones have many uses for healing and vibrational alignment. They are widely used in holistic practices among many cultures. If you choose to work on one chakra at a time the way this book is laid out, you may want to wear gemstones as jewelry to create a vibrational frequency that aligns to the energy you are moving through. However, you can use them during meditation either on an altar or placed upon the chakra you are working with. You may want to set a routine for this type of meditation or for when you are in the middle of experiencing the emotions. Setting multiple gemstones together around the house in a patterned grid amplifies the energy you are working with and creates movement of this energy. You can do this during the entire cycle of working with this chakra, then change the grid when you move to the next chakra.

Garnet: This stone connects individuals to the earth's energy. It helps establish a strong foundation and sense of stability, allowing one to feel rooted and connected to the present moment. It's the stone of energy and vitality. It helps revitalize and strengthen the physical body, promoting endurance, stamina, and a sense of motivation. It is also connected to our physical energy and survival instincts. It ignites the fire within, stimulating enthusiasm, inspiration, and a sense of purpose. Garnet can help individuals tap into their creative potential and manifest their desires. Garnet guards against negative energies, psychic attacks, and emotional draining. It can create a shield of energy, promoting a sense of security and enhancing personal power. Garnet is also believed to strengthen self-confidence, self-esteem, and self-worth.

Black tourmaline: Considered one of the most powerful protective stones, it creates an energetic shield around the wearer, deflecting and absorbing negative energies, psychic attacks, and electromagnetic radiation. It helps to create a sense of energetic boundary and protection. It helps to connect individuals to the earth's energy, promoting a sense of stability, balance, and physical well-being. It can be particularly helpful for those who feel scattered or overwhelmed, as it encourages a strong connection to the present moment. It helps cleanse and purify one's energy field as well as the surrounding environment. It absorbs and transmutes negative energies into positive, harmonious vibrations. Black tourmaline is used for emotional healing and providing a sense of calmness and stability. It helps alleviate anxiety, stress, and negative thought patterns. Black tourmaline's grounding energy can provide a sense of emotional stability and support during challenging times. It is believed to guard against psychic attacks, negative entities, and energetic attachments. Black tourmaline will aid in personal transformation and self-reflection. It assists individuals in facing and releasing deep-seated fears, limiting beliefs, and negative patterns.

Black tourmaline's energy encourages inner growth, self-empowerment, and personal development.

Ruby: This stone amplifies chi (life force energy). Ruby is often associated with passion, love, and vitality. It stimulates enthusiasm, motivation, and a zest for life. Ruby helps individuals connect with their inner desires and pursue their passions with courage and determination. It bolsters one's inner resolve, providing the energy needed to face challenges, overcome obstacles, and persevere through difficult times. Ruby is thought to enhance self-confidence and empower individuals to take bold steps toward their goals. Ruby enhances the power of affirmations and visualizations, assisting individuals in attracting their desires and creating positive changes in their lives.

Black obsidian: It helps anchor and stabilize one's energy, promoting a strong connection to the earth and a sense of stability in life. This grounding energy can assist in staying centered and balanced, especially during times of emotional turmoil or stress. Black obsidian is a powerful protective stone, particularly against negative energies and psychic attacks. It forms a shield around the aura, preventing unwanted energetic influences from entering. It also helps to absorb and transmute negative energies, promoting a purifying effect. It uncovers and brings to the surface deep-seated emotions, traumas, and blockages. By facilitating the release of these emotional patterns, black obsidian supports the process of healing and transformation. Black obsidian's reflective surface is believed to aid in self-reflection and introspection. It assists in shedding old patterns, limiting beliefs, and attachments that no longer serve one's highest good. This stone encourages self-awareness, self-acceptance, and personal evolution. It assists in accessing and understanding past-life experiences, allowing for healing and integration of relevant lessons and energies into the present life.

Red tiger's eye: Provides a boost of motivation, stamina, and endurance, making it beneficial for those needing an extra push or overcoming fatigue. It ignites a fiery energy within, stimulating enthusiasm, excitement, and a sense of drive. Helps individuals tap into their creative potential and pursue their passions. It assists in overcoming fears, boosting self-esteem, and promoting assertiveness. This stone's energy encourages taking bold actions and stepping outside of one's comfort zone. It helps establish a strong connection with the earth's energy, promoting stability and a sense of security. Red tiger's eye can support grounding and balancing energies during periods of change or stress. It enhances motivation and aids in setting and achieving goals. It helps individuals maintain focus, determination, and perseverance in their pursuits. This stone's energy encourages taking consistent action toward desired outcomes.

Red jasper: It helps individuals establish a strong connection with the earth's energy, promoting a sense of stability, security, and balance. Red jasper's grounding energy is particularly beneficial during times of change or when feeling scattered. It boosts energy levels, endurance, and overall physical well-being. Red jasper's energizing properties support the body's natural healing processes and promote stamina. It also provides a sense of comfort and grounding during challenging emotional times. Red jasper's gentle, nurturing energy promotes emotional healing, stability, and inner strength. Red jasper gives support during difficult times, helping individuals persevere and maintain a positive outlook. Red jasper's energy promotes inner strength, courage, and the ability to navigate difficulties with grace.

Coral: It alleviates stress, anxiety, and tension, allowing for emotional stability and a sense of tranquility. Coral fosters compassion, empathy, and understanding. Its energy can support healing relationships, enhancing empathy, and cultivating a loving and caring attitude. Coral's energy can help individuals connect with their physical bodies and the earth, promoting a strong foundation.

Oils and Herbs

As with gemstones, oils and herbs can be used in many ways during the healing process. I like to use these specifically during difficult times while working through each energy field. Not only can you experience moments of intense emotion, you may also experience what's called a healing crisis. Sometimes during a healing crisis it can feel like you have flu-like symptoms. This is actually the toxins leaving the body. You can experience this after a reiki session or sometimes after a yoga sequence. There are other times you may experience a healing crisis, and in these instances, I find it useful to use the oils and herbs. This is also a good time to drink the tea blends.

Sandalwood: This calming and grounding aroma helps create a serene and focused atmosphere, allowing individuals to deepen their meditation, prayer, and spiritual connection. Sandalwood has purifying properties, both energetically and physically. It is often used to cleanse sacred spaces, objects, and the aura. Burning sandalwood incense or using sandalwood essential oil helps clear negative energies and create a sacred environment. It will create a protective shield around the user, helping to maintain a sense of spiritual safety and harmony. It helps individuals stay rooted in the present moment, promoting a sense of inner calm and stability.

Frankincense: This is considered a sacred resin and is often associated with spiritual rituals and ceremonies. It is used to enhance spiritual connection and create a sacred atmosphere conducive to prayer, meditation, and spiritual practices. It clears negative energies, dispels stagnant or lower vibrations, and purifies the environment. It is a shield against negative energies, psychic attacks, and unwanted influences. Frankincense's energy provides a sense of spiritual safety and wards off malevolent forces.

Cinnamon: It is often associated with increasing vitality, motivation, and physical energy. The aroma of cinnamon is thought to uplift the spirit and provide a boost of enthusiasm. It is believed to create a shield against negative energies, harmful influences, and psychic attacks. Burning cinnamon sticks or using cinnamon essential oil is often used to purify and protect a space or an individual's energy field. Cinnamon is used in rituals, spells, or charms to enhance financial success and manifest abundance. It is used to aid in physical and emotional healing by stimulating circulation, boosting the immune system, and providing comfort during times of illness or distress. Cinnamon has aphrodisiac properties and can be used to enhance romantic relationships and kindle passion.

Palo santo: Burning palo santo wood or using palo santo essential oil clears negative energies, stagnant emotions, and unwanted influences from the environment and the energy field. It is often used to cleanse spaces, objects, and the aura. The aromatic smoke of palo santo creates a protective barrier, promoting a sense of safety and well-being. Palo santo is also known for its grounding and centering qualities. It helps individuals stay rooted in the present moment, promoting a sense of inner calm, stability, and balance. Palo santo can support grounding practices and meditation. Palo santo has healing properties on both physical and emotional levels. It relieves stress, anxiety, and emotional imbalances. Palo santo's aroma promotes relaxation, uplifts the mood, and creates a soothing environment. Its aroma stimulates the senses, awakens the mind, and encourages creative expression. Palo santo is a tool for spiritual rituals, prayers, and offerings. Its presence and fragrance elevates the sacredness of the space and enhances the overall spiritual experience. Palo santo is sacred to Indigenous people. If you choose this over the others mentioned, make sure it is ethically and sustainably sourced and supports Indigenous communities.

Nag champa: Its soothing and calming fragrance creates a serene atmosphere, helping individuals relax, focus, and deepen their spiritual connection. Burning nag champa incense helps in creating a sacred space and enhancing the spiritual experience. Nag champa is used to clear negative

energies, stagnant emotions, and promote a sense of purification in the environment. Its calming and grounding
properties help create a conducive environment for mental clarity and deep concentration. Burning nag champa
incense is used to enhance concentration during study,
work, or spiritual practices. Its aroma is believed to induce
a sense of tranquility, ease anxiety, and promote emotional well-being.

Shadow Work

If you've picked up this book, you're probably ready to make
changes in your life. Doing shadow work is recovery work, and
there is no wrong way to do it. However, I have developed a flow
that I find works successfully with my own shadow work. If you're
like me, sometimes it's hard to find the feelings or know where to
start. The following practice is how I start this work.

1. Where are your physical issues? If you have stomach
   issues, maybe start with the solar plexus. If you are not
   sure about what is physically out of alignment, I would
   simply start with the root and move up from there.

2. Once you decide which chakra you are going to start
   focusing on, put your energy and thoughts toward that
   chakra at night. Even before knowing what may come
   up, simply put your hands on that energy center as you
   fall asleep. You can send healing light visually to that
   chakra and say out loud or to yourself "I am ready to
   release any stuck and unhealed energy. I am ready to
   see what has been hiding in the shadows." Then be
   open to what happens next. Your days to follow will
   bring up issues you have been avoiding.

3. Set time aside weekly for processing the emotions, emotional reactions, triggers, and social interactions that are coming up. You may even want to do this daily before you go to bed. Start journaling the questions you are asking and answering for yourself.

4. Finally, decide which of the provided tools you will use and create a routine for each. Slowly integrate changes into your routine. Do not try to do everything all at once. In order to create sustainable lifestyle changes, you should start with one at a time. After you feel comfortable with steps two and three, maybe add drinking herbal teas or yoga once a week.

Questions for Root Chakra Shadow Work

These are the hard questions that you will need to think about in order to rewrite your foundation, the root of your vibration.

Listen to how you feel. Are you depressed, or do you disassociate and have a hard time staying present? How do you feel about your emotional experiences, and how do you cope with challenges related to staying present and connected to the present moment? Do you dissociate or fall into your routine without being aware of your surroundings? The opposite of this is hypervigilance of your surroundings. How would you describe your sense of safety and security in life? How do you perceive the balance in your life currently? And how do you experience or manage any feelings of anxiety you may have? Unstable foundational years will create feelings of imbalance and a need for survival mode to be consistently on. How do you approach acquiring and keeping materials in your life? Do you ever experience a sense of your basic human needs being under threat or in a constant state of insecurity? All of these are feelings that stem from an insecure foundation. Start to incorporate some of the tools from earlier in the chapter, like the foods, oils and herbs, gemstones, or sounds to help balance the root.

However, these tools are not enough; they are tools that will move the stuck energy from the root chakra. They will help restore balance, but just like anything in life, unless you heal the source and change the habits created from the source of imbalance, you will go right back to where you started. This is why we do shadow work.

Shadow work requires an extreme amount of honesty, and it also requires you to strengthen your listening skills. The honesty required here is with yourself. You need to be able to admit to yourself where you have abused your own characteristics.

Oftentimes, and the reason we have a shadow side, we tend to use our natural-born gifts as a weapon against our own life. For example, someone who is born with persuasive communication skills may be taught that they are manipulative instead of encouraged to become a lawyer. I've always been gifted at reading a person's emotions and knowing their weak spots and their strengths. I used this gift as a defense mechanism, a way to keep people away from me instead of learning how to use it to connect with people.

When we have created a life of survival instead of thriving, those natural-born gifts become our dark side, our shadow side. You have to bring from the shadows those parts of you that you pretend don't exist and return them to the light. You need to learn to use these character traits that have always been part of you as gifts instead of curses.

While we are becoming deeply ourselves, we show up everywhere in everyone, and it's time to start listening. Listening skills are about listening to how people respond and react to you. Our interactions show us what we are putting out into the world. We can use every interaction we have as a mirror to what is going on inside of us if we listen carefully.

Letter for Root Chakra Shadow Work

Because shadow work is a very deep and personal process, writing letters to yourself is extremely powerful. You are going deep into places you may not have ever been aware of. These letters provide personal support and direction. You are becoming you with intention and purpose.

The root chakra letter is about setting a new foundation. Let go of any fear you may have just for the moment and allow yourself to completely absorb spirit and be present, centered, and connected by focusing on your breath and present words only.

This was my letter in 2019:

Today, help me to let go of my resistance to change. Help me be open to the process. Help me believe that the place I'll be dropped off will be better than the place where I was picked up. Help me surrender, trust, and accept even if I do not understand.

Listen to the stories you tell yourself over and over again. Creating a new future requires a new narrative. It is our nature to only use what we already know as reference for what will come. This is why it is very important to learn how to see our foundation differently. What do you believe your life to be up to this point? I literally wrote a book about my trauma and held onto the story of my life being rooted in trauma until I was forty-two. Then one day, I let it go. I stopped making that my story. Ask yourself what story you are holding onto. Where do you see this story repeat over and over again: Same relationship, different face; same financial situation, different career?

Letters to Write to Yourself When Healing the Root Chakra

Think about your identifications in life. We all have things we use to identify ourselves: mother, sister, daughter, girlfriend, wife, teacher—all things I thought made me who I am. None of these are who "I am"; they are purely things I can align myself with.

What would happen if you stopped identifying with any of these? Would you die? I always identified as a Capricorn, a Pagan, a healer, a writer, a woman, a New Yorker. Groups and categories, boxes that I fit into. I identified by my last name. I did die many times over, but the only thing that truly died was my fear and the need to attach myself to an identity. What would happen if you no longer belonged to or identified with your roles and groups? The truth is, you would be set free. All identities come with limitations.

Dive into your beliefs politically, spiritually, and socially. Try to recognize these are simply that: belief systems. What do you believe and what do you know? These belief systems were created to instill some sort of order to chaos, to give people structure of living.

> *I can start over at any time. I can be whoever I want, wherever I want. I can build a strong foundation to stand on from here on out no matter how old I am or what I have been through. I am perfect and always free to reinvent myself. I am not bound by any definition or identification.*

Your stories and your identities dictate your beliefs, and you are just swimming in an ocean of mirrors reflecting back to you where you already are and what you already are and have always seen. Your foundational beliefs create the journey. Can you break free? Think about what it might feel like if you completely changed your reality, if the mirrors reflected back to you new images. The mirror neurons in our brains are extremely strong. Mirror neurons are a type of neuron that fire both when an individual performs a specific action and when they observe someone else performing the same action. They were first discovered in the 1990s and are believed to contribute to our ability to understand the intentions and emotions of others by simulating their actions in our own brain. This simulation mechanism may facilitate the learning of new skills through imitation and the development of social behavior. In other words, we learn by reflections of those we surround ourselves with.

Most of us forget whose voice we hear when we think about our beliefs. Who told you how to view the world, and how did their views affect you? These voices could be family members, spiritual leaders, or even educators. In the modern world, the voices are heavily saturated by pop culture and media. There is a reason the voices of your childhood told you to view the world the way they did. Most likely these reasons were born from survival needs, but do you have those same survival needs? This is when we begin to break generational curses. Our lives no longer resemble the lives of our ancestors. We are not having the same experience, and we are not living in the same environment. Therefore, their beliefs most likely don't fit. What would happen if you said, "Thank you, but no thank you. I am no longer looking at the world from your perspective. I choose me and my own view." Can you write letters to those people releasing their beliefs?

When doing this work in the root, you must find people who are already where you want to be. You must start to learn through the reflections of those people. This is one way you will start to change the program. Like any healing journey, you cannot stay in the same place and expect a different result. The people around you will always reflect back to you and become part of your vibration.

Affirmations for Root Chakra Energy Work

I am safe! I am supported!
I am free to choose what makes me happy every day!
I am experiencing life from pleasure and joy every day!

Recipes for Root Chakra Energy Work

For each tea blend, I use loose-leaf herbs and tea leaves and make the blends in 20-ounce Mason jars. I use about ⅓ of a cup for each ingredient. I gently roll the Mason jar to mix the ingredients together without breaking up the herbs into dust.

When I'm ready to brew the tea, I heat up water in a teapot and scoop a tablespoon of the blend into a reusable tea bag. I then add my tea bag plus other ingredients such as honey or lemon (to taste) to a mug before the water is done. When the water is hot, I add it to the mug slowly.

To activate the tea with the incantation, I do a few things: First, I will write the incantation onto a sticky note and put it on the pot as it heats the water. As I pour the water slowly, I will read the incantation out loud. I stop the pour with enough room at the top of my mug so that the next part does not cause the water to spill out. Once the water is a little cooled down, I will place my right hand over the top of the mug and grasp it (not by its handle but by the rim) so that the energy from my hand is also infused into the water. Once I have a firm grip, I will pick it up and swirl the mug and tea clockwise three times while saying the incantation. I will also repeat this on my left side three times but counterclockwise. Then I will go back to my right hand and repeat the swirl but counterclockwise then left hand clockwise.

Your tea is now fully infused with the energy you intend, and once it is cooled down enough to drink, enjoy.

Forever Young Tea and Incantation

- Hibiscus, pomegranate, vanilla bean, maca root, green tea

Or

- Butterfly pea, lemon peel, mint

"Venus, Aphrodite, and Cleopatra. Drink with me a potion of youthful herbs. Allow me to grow with little age. Restore me to your form. Make me your sage."

Fountain of Me Tea and Incantation

- Seaweed, elderberry, burdock root, wild cherry bark, nettle, mullein

"Belly full of laughs, plate full of glee. Glass full of vino, come drink with me. There's plenty for the taking, even more for creating, my house full of riches, my heart full of tea."

Movement and Yoga Sequence for the Root

Balancing your root chakra is not just about shadow work and healings. It's also about taking back your life and creating new ground for you to plant firmly into a new and bright future. Go for daily walks outside. When I do this, I visualize all of my chakras spinning and generating the ideal day, month, and year. In addition to mindful walks to stop and smell the roses, I believe in purging. Purge your body by eating clean foods that are not processed. Purge your house by throwing out everything that doesn't fit the future you.

Yoga is a practice that combines physical postures (asanas), breathing techniques (pranayama), meditation, and ethical principles, all aimed at achieving a state of alignment in the body, mind, and soul.

1. **Mountain Pose** (Tadasana):
   - Stand tall with your feet together or hip-width apart.
   - Ground down through all four corners of your feet.
   - Engage your thighs and lift your kneecaps.
   - Lengthen your spine and relax your shoulders.
   - Bring your palms together at your heart center, fingers pointing upward.

2. **Forward Fold** (Uttanasana):
   - Exhale as you hinge forward from your hips, folding your torso over your legs.
   - Keep your knees slightly bent if needed to bring your hands to the floor.
   - Relax your neck and let your head hang.

3. **Lunge:**
   - Step your right foot back, keeping your left foot grounded.
   - Bend your left knee to create a lunge position.
   - Align your front knee directly over your ankle.
   - Lift your torso, keeping your spine long and core engaged.

4. **Plank Pose:**
   - Step your left foot back to meet your right foot, coming into a high plank position.

- Align your wrists directly under your shoulders.
- Engage your core and lengthen your spine, maintaining a straight line from head to heels.
- Spread your fingers wide apart and press your palms into the mat.

5. **Warrior I (Virabhadrasana I):**
   - From plank pose, step your right foot forward between your hands.
   - Rotate your back foot to a 45-degree angle, grounding it firmly.
   - Bend your right knee, keeping it directly over your ankle.
   - Lift your torso, extending your arms overhead with your palms facing each other.
   - Gaze forward or slightly upward, maintaining a strong and stable lower body.

6. **Triangle Pose (Utthita Trikonasana):**
   - Straighten your right leg, keeping your feet in the same position.
   - Extend your arms out to the sides at shoulder height.
   - Hinge at your right hip, reaching your right hand toward your right foot.
   - Rest your right hand on your shin, ankle, or the floor (use a block if needed).
   - Extend your left arm straight up, creating a straight line from your left hand to your right foot.
   - Gaze at your left hand or toward the ceiling.

7. **Yogi Squat (Malasana):**

- From triangle pose, release your right hand to the floor or a block.

- Bend both knees and lower your hips down toward the ground.

- Bring your palms together at your heart center, using your elbows to gently press your knees apart.

- Keep your spine long and your chest lifted.

8. **Child's Pose (Balasana):**

- Come to an all-fours position with your knees hip-width apart.

- Lower your hips back onto your heels.

- Walk your hands forward, extending your arms in front of you.

- Rest your forehead on the mat and relax your entire body.

- Take deep breaths and surrender to the pose.

9. **Corpse Pose (Savasana):**

- Lie flat on your back, allowing your legs and arms to relax by your sides.

- Close your eyes and let go of any tension in your body.

- Soften your breath and allow yourself to completely surrender.

- Stay in this pose for a few minutes, focusing on relaxation and deep rest.

Remember to listen to your body and modify the poses as needed. It's always important to practice yoga mindfully and honor your individual limitations. If you're new to yoga or have any specific concerns, it's a good idea to seek guidance from a qualified yoga instructor.

Enjoy your practice!

Meditations

The first meditation you will learn and practice is the foundation to every other meditation in this book. I will reference back to it in each chapter. Practicing this simple meditation alone will have a profound impact on your life. Tip: Try to have a meditation spot that stays the same—keep the music the same, the incense the same. Most divination tools can change, but always start with centering and bringing the light down from the soul star to the core of the earth and back up around you. This will create memory within your body, mind, and soul. You are training yourself to release thoughts and just be.

Centering and Grounding Yourself

Find music that you feel aligned to and will want to incorporate into your meditation practice every time. Visualize or actually be outdoors. The best place would be in the center of a sacred circle. Close your eyes with your feet flat on the ground if you are sitting in a chair, uncrossed if you are lying down. Visualize white light (soul star energy) pouring in through the top of your mind, opening and expanding your crown chakra. Allow this liquid light of healing to release all thoughts. Feel your mind become quiet and soft. Release your facial muscles, eyes, jaw.

Visualize your third eye and pineal gland opening and releasing old energy and becoming renewed with clear sight. Let the white light pour down your spine, opening your throat chakra, relaxing your shoulders. Feel the energy slowly move down your arms, relaxing every muscle. Feel your arms soften as the energy moves past your elbows, releasing tension in your wrists and activating your palm chakras.

Feel this white light opening and healing your heart chakra, allowing your back muscles to fully relax, sinking deeper into healing. Feel the energy move down into your solar plexus, healing your organs and cleansing your body. The energy slowly moves into your sacral, activating inspiration and creativity. Feel the white healing light open your root chakra, releasing tension in your hips and relaxing your thigh muscles. Move down toward your feet, releasing tension in your calves and ankles. Feel this beautiful light activate the chakras in the soles of your feet.

The energy then moves toward the heart of Gaia, connecting and grounding you to your earth chakra. Visualize this healing light coming up through the ground, surrounding you in light and burning away attachments that no longer serve you. This energy moves through every layer of your aura, cleansing and activating each. The light soon reaches the Merkabah above your crown chakra, completing the circle of light and activating your astral body.

The term *Merkabah* is Hebrew and refers to a divine, spiritual chariot or vehicle that serves as a means of transportation for ascended beings or the soul. The Merkabah involves meditative techniques, prayers, and visualizations aimed at ascending to higher spiritual realms and experiencing a direct connection with the Divine. It looks like a three-dimensional, six-pointed star: two pyramids combined.

As your physical body stays in healing, your astral body travels to your personal sanctuary, a place between worlds that connects you to your guides and soul. Your soul has traveled here with each passing of lives to rest and learn. Take a moment to look around your sanctuary and get reacquainted with this space, as you have been here many times. See yourself as the center. In your mind, allow the sacred circle to become a garden and just observe the stages of living and dying among this garden. Try to feel the air, hear the wind, and smell the earth. Be present as the sacred circle breathes and grows around you.

When using just the grounding and centering meditation alone and not in conjunction with other visualizations, you don't necessarily need to "exit" the meditation. You sit with the energy for as long as you like: five, ten, twenty minutes, or however long, and when you are ready, you simply feel the physical again. You take a moment to feel your toes all the way up to your mind. This healing light and grounding meditation is a great energy system to incorporate into your daily life.

The Rose Garden

This next meditation and all others will be a continuation of the grounding and centering meditation you just practiced. After the light is around you and you find yourself in the sanctuary at the center, I want you to notice a bookshelf. The bookshelf keeps all references for you that you will need along the journey in the body. You may want to visit and check things out at a later time.

See the doors on each side of the bookshelf. Today, you will be going through the door to the left. Standing in front of the door is a guardian. They are there to greet you and give you messages that you may need for today's visit. As you approach, you are greeted, and once the message (if any) is received, the door will open.

On the other side of the door is a rose garden. You will be entering through a path of roses on the east side of this circle.

Walk right to the center and take a look around. I want you to notice what lies in each direction of the garden. Look to the south, and in your mind record what you see. Look to the west, then north, and lastly east. Notice the colors of the roses, the stages of life they are in, and take note of any animals that may be present or guides from the celestial realm.

Beyond the rose garden is a forest, and beyond that is a place meant for you made up of your life's purpose. As you practice this meditation, you will be guided by spirit through different areas of this realm in order to guide your soul. Here in the rose garden, you may ask any questions you want. This is the place that holds the answers to very specific events currently happening in your timeline's reality. You may receive the answers through the roses, through other objects that appear in the garden, by walking beyond the garden, or by listening and conversing with guides. You will know your journey in the rose garden is complete for the day because you will receive the answers you need to hear.

Keep in mind that they will tell you what you need to hear, not what you may want to hear. They may show you things that will surprise you or give you direction you may be avoiding. The rose garden is a direct connection to your life's path and a way to walk the path with greater clarity and at your fullest vibration. When the journey is complete, walk back through the east side of the circle, exiting the way you came in and walking back through the door to your sanctuary. Find the couch in your sanctuary and allow the visions of the room to dissipate, only seeing yourself surrounded by white light. Start to feel your physical body back in the room where you began the meditation. Feel your body from your toes to your head and every part in between. You will notice you feel heavy, present, and maybe a little dense again. At this point, you may open your eyes.

You may have received messages and visions while on your journey. You may want to write them down in a journal or just take mental notes. Sometimes they have an immediate impact, and other times they may be future realities and not make sense at the moment. I always try to record my visions and messages. I find that even if they have immediately impacted my life, there is always more to come. Pay attention to your own mind and thoughts, and remind yourself as often as necessary to look toward and focus on things that make you happy. Consciously move your thoughts toward things that make you happy, and feel the goodness as much as you can. When you feel good, then visualize the life you want for yourself.

The Root Activation

Activating each chakra means acknowledging it and turning it on to its highest potential. Essentially, you are creating a union or a relationship with each chakra during the activating.

For this practice, you're going to create a circle similar to the one in the rose garden meditation; however, this will be a real circle outside among the garden or trees or even on the beach—wherever you choose. The only requirement for placement is that you feel comfortable to sit there and meditate. I like to build it either in my own yard or in a place I know very few people visit. I like to actually build the circle on my birthday and then come back to it as often as needed during the year. I build the circle during my birthday because in my tradition it is believed that the things you do on the three days of your birthday (the day before, the day of, and the day after) are very important days that create the manifestations of the coming year. Also, we are working with the root chakra here, which is about self-identity and a strong foundation, so if your birthday is coming up, it would be a great time to do this. But it's doable anytime.

You will start by collecting rocks, either anytime during the year or the days around your birthday. For this part, the only thing that matters is that you are using stones native to the land you will be building the circle on. You will need at least seventy-two stones roughly around the same size and five slightly bigger or much bigger stones. You will use the bigger stones to sit next to or, depending on size, possibly sit on them.

Once the stones are collected, gather them in the place you will build the circle. Locate east, south, west, and north. The east is always your starting point. You can think of this as the circle gate. Then place, in this order, four of the large stones, one in each of the four directions. Start in the east and walk to the south in a curved line in order to create a circle. You want the circle to be large enough that you can sit inside it in any direction. Once you place the stone at the north, you will continue back to the east stone, completing the circle.

Next, you will place nine smaller stones between each of the larger stones (totaling thirty-six stones that represent the path of life), again starting at the east and walking the circle in a clockwise direction. Once you again return to the east, you will use your remaining stones to create a line of nine stones from each direction straight to the center of the circle. Complete this at the north, then again walk back to the east. Finally, you will take the last remaining large stone and place it directly into the center of the circle where all four lines meet. In order to exit the circle, always walk from where you are in a clockwise direction until you get to the east, and there you may exit.

Entering in from the east is representative of rebirth, the sunrise, and new beginnings. You will sit in the east of the circle while meditating or doing ritual if you believe you are at the beginning of a new chapter or need a fresh start. The element of air is the medicine in the east; you can use wind chimes to represent ringing in your new life. Air is connected to the breath of life and can be used in times when communication is needed.

The south is the element of fire. Sit in the south of the circle when looking for inspiration, creativity, and to rise up again. Fire is also purifying and can be used to release old patterns and behaviors and make room for a new, youthful journey. Burn candles when utilizing the energy of the south to light the fire within.

The west is water and represents your emotions. Sit here when you want to gain emotional wisdom and strength and when you want to get clarity on what it is you are feeling and cleanse out the old emotions. The west, and the water it represents, can help create a gentle flow. Meditate here when you want to connect with the flow of source energy. This is a great time to use moon water for your intentions and emotions. Call upon the direction of the west to aid in the flow of your magic.

The north is the element of earth. Sit in the north when you want to call upon strength, stability, prosperity, and wisdom. I like to use my herbs and plants when I am using the magic of the north. The north is where you can also access the higher knowledge of ancestors and the Divine.

The center of the circle is mostly where I like to sit, but this is only because I do a lot of listening. Oftentimes I do not know what I need, and the center is the soul of the circle, the place where you can access your personal guides and light. I set up each direction with air, fire, water, and earth, then make my way to the soul or the center rock to sit upon. I close my eyes and ask for guidance. It took me many, many years of practice before I understood how to fully access my guides.

Now, when I sit in the center, I ask for guidance on specific things, such as relationships, career, health, etc. Often, I understand exactly what the truth is. I have been told to throw out the old skin suit and start again. I have been told I must let people go. I have been told that others will choose me, that contracts will be signed or broken. It's the center of this circle that I now know is where the true listening is. It is the soul.

I think the best way to practice this connection is to sit within the center of the circle and do the first meditation mentioned in this chapter, centering and grounding. Then allow yourself to just listen and visualize. Don't get me wrong, I still use each element and portion of the circle, but these are for very specific moments when I need an extra push into the energy.

Ritual

The root chakra ritual is all about rewriting your reality, or, I like to say, creating a new foundation without attachments. We want to achieve a foundation that is sturdy and in total alignment to the real you.

Letters to Me

Buy as many greeting cards as you want. These will all be written to yourself. Starting today, write yourself a card imagining all the good feelings you want in your life. Write broadly what you want it to look like. This is not a vision board; it is not supposed to be specific. This is just the emotions you want to manifest in your life and build from.

> *Example:* "I am happy working with people to help them heal. I am safe with a circle of family and friends who support me and feel supported by me."

Keep it about the basics and the simple things without painting a picture of what that may look like. I used this technique in my life, and one of the things I included was, "I will grow younger." My intent was to create a healthy, sustainable lifestyle to promote longevity. What I got was a relationship with an age gap that kept me young and helped me keep myself accountable to these goals. I was open to whatever it might look like, and when I opened that card a year later, I had gotten exactly what I wanted.

Seal up the card and write today's date on the back. Hide this card somewhere in your home, a book you haven't read in a while, a drawer you don't often go into, somewhere you may otherwise lose stuff. You will forget you wrote this card to yourself. When the time is right, the card will find you, and when you open this card, you will be surprised to find everything you wrote has now come true in your life. Do this as often as you feel you need to in order to remind yourself to focus on the feelings you want.

Psychic Center of the Root

Each chakra has a superpower that you can access when you have begun to clear out the blocks and heal the energy. I call these the psychic centers for each chakra because you can become open to processes that go beyond the realm of the ordinary. Gaining access to these connections in your energy system will have a continued effect on your healing.

Kundalini refers to the primal energy that resides at the base of the spine, often depicted as a coiled serpent. In Kundalini yoga and various other spiritual traditions, the awakening and activation of this dormant energy is seen as a path to spiritual growth, transformation, and enlightenment. Kundalini is a powerful, dormant energy that lies coiled at the base of the spine, specifically in the area known as the muladhara or root chakra. It is considered the source of spiritual awakening and holds the potential for expanded consciousness. Kundalini is closely associated with the chakra system. The awakened Kundalini energy moves through each chakra, bringing balance, healing, and spiritual awareness. Although Kundalini begins in the root chakra, it should not be explored until you are ready. The Kundalini experience is a very powerful one that you may want to experience further down your spiritual journey. Taking a class is good place to start when you are ready. You can do Kundalini at any point in your journey, and it doesn't need to happen during this phase of your healing. I suggest you move through each chakra at least once and then come back and explore Kundalini.

Chapter Three
Sacral Chakra, Svadhisthana

Located at the center of the pelvis a few inches below the navel, this energy center balances your sexual energy. This is not only referring to the act of having sex or sex organs like the root, but the energy of flow, inspiration, and creation. This energy center is mostly where we live and, in my opinion, most often out of balance and most important to create a life you truly enjoy. When balanced, it keeps us in an energy of faith instead of fear, and it allows us to be productive in our endeavors and creates a powerful flow of attraction in all ways. The sacral is where we balance intimacy, emotions, relationships, and healthy sexuality.

We can look at it as how we connect to God and also as the source of original "sin," pain, or fear. The sacral holds the energy of the umbilical cord. In the womb, we are connected to our creator, and suddenly we are disconnected once we are born. This is one reason why skin to skin is very important in an infant's life. They will be comforted knowing that their creator is still present and hasn't abandoned them.

The sacral starts to develop during puberty. Things we experience during this time either enhance our passions and creativity or inhibit them. We start to learn about trust in the self. The way we are nurtured creates a healthy environment for self-trust or a toxic environment where we question our own actions and choices. There are many ways to correct a blocked sacral and allow the life force energy to flow in harmony with your energy system.

I Feel

The sacral chakra is related to all that we feel emotionally. "I feel" expresses this. We all feel, but oftentimes we don't allow ourselves to truly comprehend what it is we are feeling. By using the term "I feel," it starts the process of giving ourselves permission to feel even before we know what exactly it is we feel. We have created hundreds of programs just to understand what it is we are feeling. Giving ourselves permission to feel our feelings will then help guide us to the resources we need to identify our feelings.

Our society has programmed us to remove ourselves from feeling. We no longer trust our own internal sense of emotions. The sacral chakra is, in my opinion, the most important energy center for psychic abilities and manifesting the life you want. When we are in alignment with our flow of emotions and trust "our gut," we can flow easily within our own life and decisions. We can stay present in the moment and allow the future to grow from the now. We can "feel" life.

Tools and Properties of the Sacral for Alignment

Emotional connections: Sexual desires, intimacy, pleasure, creativity/the creator, inspiration, victimhood, issues of the woman/motherhood, goddess development, separateness from others, self, and God

Physical connections: Hips, intestines, fallopian tubes, ovaries, genitals, reproductive organs, glands, bladder, urinary tract, kidneys, lower spine, pelvis

Foods: Sweet potatoes, salmon, carrots, apricots, peaches, oranges

Activities: Healthy sexual activity, dancing, style (allowing yourself to freely express an outward appearance)

Color: Orange—The sacral responds to an orange vibration, all things that have absorbed the earth's and sun's combination of orange rays and minerals. The sacral balances when fed orange foods.

Element: Water—Taking a bath or swimming in the ocean or any natural body of water cleanses and balances your sacral energy. Drinking enough water each day is important as well. When you stand in the shower, you can tell yourself, "I allow my emotions to process through me easily without getting stuck."

Tones and notes: D, oh—Listening to music, sounds, and frequencies that have these in them can break up blocks and clear out energy in the sacral. Sounds can be a very healing tool for anyone to use. Attend a sound healing class or listen to frequencies on any music app.

Gemstones

Gemstones have many uses for healing and vibrational alignment. They are widely used in holistic practices among many cultures. If you choose to work on one chakra at a time the way this book is laid out, you may want to wear gemstones as jewelry to create a vibrational frequency that aligns to the energy you are moving through. However, you can use them during meditation either on an altar or placed upon the chakra you are working with. You may want to set a routine for this type of meditation or for when you are in the middle of experiencing the emotions. Setting multiple gemstones together around the house in a patterned grid amplifies the energy you are working with and creates movement of this energy. You can do this during the entire cycle of working with this chakra, then change the grid when you move to the next chakra.

Carnelian: This stone invigorates the body, mind, and spirit, promoting a sense of motivation, courage, and determination. Carnelian's vibrant energy is thought to awaken and activate one's life force. Carnelian stimulates the creative flow, enhances artistic expression, and fuels the imagination. Carnelian's energy is used to overcome creative blocks and bring forth new ideas and innovative thinking. Carnelian boosts self-esteem, courage, and assertiveness. Carnelian's energy can help individuals overcome self-doubt, embrace their personal power, and take bold action in their lives. Despite its fiery energy, carnelian helps individuals stay anchored in the present moment, promoting a sense of stability, security, and balance. Carnelian enhances focus, drive, and ambition, supporting individuals in achieving their goals. Carnelian's energy attracts opportunities, abundance, and positive outcomes. Carnelian enhances one's connection to their inner self, spiritual guides, and higher realms. Carnelian's energy can support the flow of creative and sexual energies, as well as facilitate a deeper understanding of one's emotions and desires.

Orange agate: This stone provides a sense of balance and stability to the wearer or the environment. Agate's grounding energy can help individuals stay rooted in the present moment, promoting a sense of calm and security. Agate balances yin and yang energies within the body, promoting harmony and equilibrium. Agate's energy can help balance emotions, thoughts, and energies, allowing for greater overall well-being. Soothing and calming, agate helps reduce stress and anxiety and promotes a sense of tranquility. Agate's energy can aid in relaxation, fostering a peaceful state of mind and emotional well-being. It also supports physical health, aids in the healing process, and boosts the immune system. Agate's energy can also assist in grounding and balancing the body's energy systems.

Orange calcite: This stone's vibrant energy awakens the imagination, encourages innovative thinking, and supports artistic endeavors. Orange calcite can help overcome creative blocks and ignite a passion for self-expression. Orange calcite promotes a positive outlook, boosts mood, and brings about a sense of happiness. Orange calcite's energy can help dispel feelings of depression, sadness, or anxiety and bring about a renewed sense of optimism. Orange calcite provides a revitalizing boost, increases vitality, and stimulates action. Orange calcite is associated with creativity, emotions, and personal relationships. It activates and balances a healthy flow of energy, enhanced intuition, and the ability to connect with one's emotions and desires.

Sunstone: This stone connects with the energy of the sun, bringing about warmth, light, and vitality. Sunstone's energy can help rejuvenate the spirit, boost energy levels, and bring about a sense of enthusiasm and optimism. Sunstone strengthens one's sense of self, promotes self-worth, and encourages assertiveness. Sunstone's energy can help individuals overcome self-doubt, embrace their inner strength, and express themselves with clarity and conviction. It is associated with joy and positivity. Sunstone uplifts the mood, dispels negativity, and brings about a sense of happiness and contentment. Sunstone helps manifest one's desires and attracts opportunities for success and prosperity. It is associated with the sacral and solar plexus chakras, promoting vitality, creativity, and personal power. Sunstone's energy can help balance and align the chakras, facilitating the free flow of energy throughout the body.

Amber: This stone has a warm and nurturing energy that helps to cleanse and purify the body, mind, and spirit. Amber's energy assists in physical healing, boosts vitality, and promotes overall well-being. Amber helps alleviate stress, anxiety, and emotional turmoil. Amber's gentle vibration can promote a sense of inner peace, relaxation, and emotional balance. Amber brings about a sense of comfort, happiness, and inner radiance. Amber's energy can help uplift the mood, enhance creativity, and promote a positive attitude.

Oils and Herbs

As with gemstones, oils and herbs can be used in many ways during the healing process. I like to use these specifically during difficult times while working through each energy field. Not only can you experience moments of intense emotion, you may also experience what's called a healing crisis. Sometimes during a healing crisis it can feel like you have flu-like symptoms. This is actually the toxins leaving the body. You can experience this after a reiki session or sometimes after a yoga sequence. There are other times you may experience a healing crisis, and in these instances, I find it useful to use the oils and herbs. This is also a good time to drink the tea blends.

Ylang-ylang: This sweet and floral fragrance has a soothing effect on the mind and body, promoting relaxation and reducing stress and anxiety. It balances mood swings, reduces feelings of sadness or anger, and promotes emotional well-being. Ylang-ylang has the ability to enhance sensuality and intimacy. Its fragrance is believed to stimulate passion, enhance the connection between partners, and create a romantic atmosphere. Ylang-ylang is used to promote new love and connection, and it enhances sexual energy and relationships. Ylang-ylang boosts self-esteem, enhances self-worth, and encourages self-acceptance. Ylang-ylang's aroma can inspire a sense of self-love and appreciation. Ylang-ylang's energy can promote the flow of energy and bring about a sense of balance and alignment. It helps stimulate adrenal glands and is calming and relaxing.

Jasmine: This aroma is believed to awaken the senses, enhance intimacy, and promote feelings of passion and desire. Jasmine's energy can inspire a deeper connection between partners and create a romantic and loving atmosphere. Jasmine has properties that support self-love and confidence. Its fragrance boosts self-esteem, fosters self-acceptance, and inspires a sense of inner beauty. Jasmine's energy can help individuals embrace their uniqueness, develop self-confidence, and cultivate a loving relationship with themselves. Jasmine clears negative energies, cleanses the aura, and creates a sacred space. Jasmine's energy can help ward off negativity, enhance spiritual protection, and promote a sense of safety and well-being. Jasmine's energy is believed to align with the law of attraction, helping individuals manifest their desires and attract prosperity and success. Jasmine's energy can support intention setting, positive affirmations, and the manifestation of goals and dreams.

Hibiscus: This plant has the ability to bloom and flourish even in challenging conditions and is considered a representation of resilience and personal evolution. Hibiscus can serve as a reminder to embrace change, adapt to new circumstances, and embrace personal growth. Hibiscus's vibrant colors and alluring appearances can symbolize romantic love, desire, and sensuality. Hibiscus can be used in rituals and practices focused on attracting love, deepening existing relationships, or cultivating self-love. Hibiscus is admired for its natural beauty and elegance. Its enchanting blossoms are often seen as a representation of external and internal beauty. Hibiscus can remind us to appreciate the beauty in ourselves, others, and the world around us. It encourages us to embrace our unique qualities and radiate grace and charm. Hibiscus represents qualities such as nurturing, intuition, and creativity. Hibiscus can be used in rituals or meditations to connect with the feminine aspects of ourselves and the universe as well as tapping into our intuition and embracing our creative potential.

Raspberry leaf: Revered as an herb that supports women's health and reproductive well-being, raspberry leaf is believed to connect individuals with the energy of the divine feminine, promoting inner strength, balance, and empowerment. It is associated with the energy of Mother Earth and the nurturing qualities of the natural world. Raspberry leaf is believed to offer a sense of protection, both spiritually and energetically, fostering a safe and supportive environment. Raspberry leaf represents the cycles of life, growth, and renewal. Raspberry leaf is believed to help individuals reconnect with the natural world, tap into its wisdom, and gain a deeper appreciation for the earth's abundant offerings. It helps individuals feel more rooted and centered, especially during times of change or emotional turbulence. Raspberry leaf's energy can bring a sense of stability, grounding, and balance to the spiritual and emotional aspects of life. Raspberry leaf supports the body's natural healing processes and promotes overall well-being. Raspberry leaf's energy can facilitate spiritual healing, renewal, and rejuvenation, allowing individuals to release what no longer serves them and embrace new beginnings. It helps reduce inflammation, boosts the immune system, and promotes healthy digestion and pregnancy.

Damiana: This plant enhances love energies and romantic connections. It stimulates passion, sensuality, and desire. Damiana can be used to create a loving and intimate atmosphere and enhance the spiritual connection between partners. Damiana is known for its mood-enhancing properties. It is believed to uplift the spirits, promote relaxation, and reduce stress and anxiety. Damiana is seen as an herb that enhances spiritual energy and vitality. It strengthens the connection to the spiritual realm, increases spiritual awareness, and promotes a sense of aliveness. Damiana amplifies intentions, aids in manifesting desires, and boosts self-assurance. Damiana's energy can support the manifestation of goals, enhance manifestation practices, and cultivate a positive mindset.

Lemongrass: This scent is believed to clear negative energies, dispel stagnant or heavy vibrations, and create a fresh and uplifting environment. Lemongrass can be used in smoke cleansing rituals, baths, or as an incense to purify the energy of spaces and individuals. Lemongrass is associated with promoting positive energy and joy. Its uplifting fragrance is believed to elevate mood, increase optimism, and bring about a sense of happiness. Lemongrass can be used in rituals or aromatherapy or simply diffused in the air to create a cheerful and harmonious atmosphere. Lemongrass is associated with connecting to nature and earth energies. It is believed to promote a sense of grounding, balance, and harmony with the natural world. Lemongrass can be used to foster a deeper connection to the earth's energies and facilitate a greater appreciation for the beauty and wisdom of nature. Lemongrass enhances one's ability to manifest desires, creates positive intentions, and attracts prosperity. Lemongrass can be used in manifestation rituals, affirmations, or visualizations to support the manifestation process.

Coriander: This herb promotes feelings of love, compassion, and unity. Coriander's energy can help foster loving relationships, heal emotional wounds, and bring about a sense of harmony in one's life and surroundings. Coriander attracts good fortune, success, and financial prosperity. Its energy can be used in abundance rituals, manifestation practices, or intention setting to invite abundance into one's life.

Shadow Work

The following practice is the flow I like to use when doing my own shadow work. There is no wrong way. Find what works for you and move at your own pace.

1. Where are your physical issues? If you have stomach issues, maybe start with the solar plexus. If you are not sure about what is physically out of alignment, I would simply start with the root and move up from there.

2. Once you decide which chakra you are going to start focusing on, put your energy and thoughts toward that chakra at night. Even before knowing what may come up, simply put your hands on that energy center as you fall asleep. You can send healing light visually to that chakra and say out loud or to yourself "I am ready to release any stuck and unhealed energy. I am ready to see what has been hiding in the shadows." Then be open to what happens next. Your days to follow will bring up issues you have been avoiding.

3. Set time aside weekly for processing the emotions, emotional reactions, triggers, and social interactions that are coming up. You may even want to do this daily before you go to bed. Start journaling the questions you are asking and answering for yourself.

4. Finally, decide which of the provided tools you will use and create a routine for each. Slowly integrate changes into your routine. Do not try to do everything all at once. In order to create sustainable lifestyle changes, you should start with one at a time. After you feel comfortable with steps two and three, maybe add drinking herbal teas or yoga once a week.

Questions for Sacral Chakra Shadow Work

The questions that you have to ask for the sacral chakra might be some of the toughest questions you'll ask yourself when healing and aligning both sides of your power, light and dark. The sacral chakra is the power center of the body.

Ask yourself what some of your coping skills are when you feel out of control, when you feel your impulses taking over, when you feel afraid, when you feel anxious. What do you turn to as a coping skill—sex, drugs, adventure? How do you ignore your feelings? Have you ever taken the time to sit with the pain, the grief, the abandonment, the loss of trust and faith in yourself?

How do you tend to respond when you're feeling out of control in your life? How would you describe your ability to identify and understand your emotions? How do you typically decide what to wear when leaving the house, and what factors influence your choice? How do you approach decision-making, and do you often seek input from others to make choices?

An unbalanced or unhealed sacral chakra will create a lot of codependency issues for you in your life. With most of my clients, I recommend going to a CoDA meeting (Co-Dependents Anonymous, a 12-step program) or reading literature on codependency when we notice there are a lot of unresolved blocks around the sacral. There is one pdf on the CoDA website that I highly recommend when dealing with issues in the sacral. It is called "Recovery Patterns of Codependence," and reading this will open up an understanding to your own wounds within relationships.

We say in any 12-step program, "You have to do the work." Well, what does that actually mean, aside from reading the literature and filling out all the workbooks? They don't tell you in any of these meetings, and therefore I had to discover for myself what "the work" is. Shadow work—going deep into the parts of yourself that you have pushed aside, ignored, or even lied about—is the work. When I discovered shadow work, I began to recover all parts of who I am. I often tell my clients that recovery is only 50 percent completed on your own. The other 50 percent comes when you go back out into the wild: dating, family interactions, or simple socializing. It happens when you are put in a familiar situation and you are faced with similar decisions and reactions. How will you show up for yourself? How will you create new patterns and behaviors? I like to tell my clients that you can't create the future from what you know because all you know relies on the past. You have to be willing to venture into the unknown in order to create a life you've never lived before.

This work requires an extreme amount of patience with yourself and a willingness to dissolve old habits. It requires you to trust your new awareness, and with that you build trust back into yourself. This time when you are faced with a dynamic that once catapulted you into a panic attack, you can stop to observe and make new, safer choices for yourself. However, because the sacral is such a powerhouse of energy, it's not enough to just stop at trusting ourselves. That is the first step that you need to build upon. Once you slowly start to build trust, you start to feel creative again. You feel like you can take risks in the production of your life. You start to feel like you can live those pipe dreams, and you start to believe in yourself. This is when the power of manifestation starts to creep in—when you believe you can create anything.

This is when magic really starts to happen, and later you will see how each chakra is connected and important and powerful. But for now, stay with the sacral. The sacral is where life is created. It is where we have original fear, our separation from God. If we look at this energy center and the sexual power that becomes the creator, we know that all things originate from this energy. We put our life into motion through passion and inspiration.

Body dysmorphia is another symptom of an imbalanced chakra. No matter what your body looks like, if you can enjoy it, be proud of it, and allow it to move, you are in balance with your God energy. Dancing is the best activity for this; however, the yoga sequence that I will provide will also help balance this chakra.

Balancing the sacral chakra requires an honest amount of vulnerability. You need to be able to admit your feelings. You need to be able to release those feelings in a healthy way. There is a program I became certified in back in the '90s called Primal Emotional Energy Release, and the whole idea behind this practice is to "hit the pillow"—to express your feelings physically in a safe, healthy environment. This is extremely important when dealing with the sacral energy source. If you're like me, when your feelings get too intense, you freeze up. This leads to an enormous amount of energy pent up in the body, which will find its way out and often not in very safe ways.

You have to address all of those toxic "coping" skills and turn them into productive uses of the energy. You need to learn to use the energy of the sacral in ways that continue to inspire you and encourage a building of self-trust so that you can become the producer of your own life.

When in balance, you will feel not only your feelings but your body talking to you. You will know with clarity and certainty that you just got a nauseous feeling because you are in a bad situation. You will no longer doubt that it is a trauma response, that the warning signal is real. When you become in tune with your body, your psychic abilities increase. You will no longer doubt your gut, and you will be able to act accordingly.

How do you behave? What do you believe are your personal characteristics? Do you find out about yourself through astrology, Human Design, Enneagrams, therapy, psychology, philosophy, or just personal observation?

My mother is an astrologer and has been my entire life. Growing up I was told, "Oh, you do that because you're a Capricorn" or "That's your Taurus Moon." I even knew about my rising sign, Scorpio, way before it became trendy. Astrology was my version of many kids' church experiences. I listened to her sermons about who I was and how I was supposed to live, and I ignored it all. Trine this, square that—it went in one ear and out the other. Who actually listened to their parents as a teenager?

No matter how I was being defined, I didn't like it. I had some deep-rooted anger toward stereotypes, even astrological ones, but it was the only way I knew how to see myself. As years went by, I started to pick up identifiers for my behaviors or characteristics through online personality tests and therapy. There were many diagnoses that I acquired. However, once I started really looking at my energy in its purest forms, I learned that I could balance each of these diagnoses within my personal flow of energy. I still experience highs and lows, but I no longer attach myself to those moments. I know how to regulate, and I know what my body needs in order to process and flow again.

I stopped making excuses for my behaviors or my character and simply started embracing each one. Sometimes we have to be willing to be alone as well. Sit with the discomfort that is showing up without feedback and recognize when it's time to allow yourself the feedback. Feedback is much different than social distractions. I have had two very significant relationships in my life, both pretty extreme and both toxic. When the first one ended, I screamed and cried and threw public temper tantrums about how he did me wrong. I pointed and blamed and became the best victim I could be. The second one was equally toxic, but this time during each manipulation and deceit, I looked at my part. How was I reacting? What could I do better to keep his depression and fear out of my energy? In the first relationship, I looked at him; in the second relationship, I looked at me. I learned so much over the last seven years observing my own cycles and broken pieces.

Because I had taken the time during the second relationship to look at myself as a partner, the ending didn't hurt the way most do. I never felt like I was losing a piece of myself. As a matter of fact, I felt like I had gained myself and filled holes within me, returning me back to a true connection with the sacral or God energy. I was able to see the breakup as another chapter in my life instead of another failure. It's quite astounding honestly to be able to look back at something and feel no remorse or regret at its ending. I still had to reset my nervous system, but the conscious awareness was amazing and beautiful.

Ask yourself today: Do you feel connected to energy, to people, to yourself, to God, to joy? That is what is stored in your sacral chakra. Can you let go of how you once identified yourself and rewrite your energy? One reason why I stopped going to CoDA meetings was because, just like any 12-step meeting, they open with claiming to be codependent. I no longer claim to be codependent. That was a version of me that no longer lives.

Letter for Sacral Chakra Shadow Work

During any or all new moons, write your thirty-day intention. (What do you want to focus on, change, or heal during the cycle of new moon to new moon?) Keep it simple at first until you start to see some progress in old habits being released and new, healthy habits coming in. Here's an example.

*Tonight, I feel the emotions that have caused me to use relation-
ships in order to fill my abandonment. I recognize when I'm acting in ways that don't serve my higher purpose, and I change
those old habits. I feel inspired and motivated to move forward.*

Letters to Write to Yourself When Healing the Sacral Chakra

If I could be anything, what would I be?

*If you are reading this book, then I have accomplished the "any-
thing I could be": a writer. In my life I was terrible at grammar,
still am. I had remedial English in college, and even though I have
a bunch of degrees, I still need people to correct my grammar and
spelling. In third grade we had a written survey asking us what
we liked most in school. I wrote "speling." That's right, I spelled it
wrong. What I truly liked and didn't know at the time was writing. If I could be anything, I would be a writer.*

Tell yourself you can be anything because you can, no matter
what the world has told you. Or, when they derail you from your
passion, you can always get back on track. It's not about the imagery of our desires either. It's about the feeling and the doing. I have
written a million books over the course of my life. The one you
are reading today is not one I thought I'd produce. It was never
about the book. It's always been about the feeling of having something to write. Once I realized that, I became who I am—who I
always knew I was—a writer. The sacral chakra is all about feeling, inspiration, trust, and manifesting. The God chakra! Go and
be your own creator.

Affirmations for Sacral Chakra Energy Work

I feel creative and inspired!

I trust myself and have faith that life will work out for me!

Recipes for Sacral Chakra Energy Work

For each tea blend, I use loose-leaf herbs and tea leaves and make the blends in 20-ounce Mason jars. I use equal parts of each ingredient, and I have listed about ⅓ of a cup for each ingredient. I gently roll the Mason jar to mix the ingredients together without breaking up the herbs into dust.

When I'm ready to brew the tea, I heat up water in a teapot and scoop a tablespoon of the blend into a reusable tea bag. I then add my tea bag plus other ingredients such as honey or lemon (to taste) to a mug before the water is done. When the water is hot, I add it to the mug slowly.

To activate the tea with the incantation, I do a few things: First, I will write the incantation onto a sticky note and put it on the pot as it heats the water. As I pour the water slowly, I will read the incantation out loud. I stop the pour with enough room at the top of my mug so that the next part does not cause the water to spill out. Once the water is a little cooled down, I will place my right hand over the top of the mug and grasp it (not by its handle but by the rim) so that the energy from my hand is also infused into the water. Once I have a firm grip, I will pick it up and swirl the mug and tea clockwise three times while saying the incantation. I will also repeat this on my left side three times but counterclockwise. Then I will go back to my right hand and repeat the swirl but counterclockwise then right hand clockwise.

Your tea is now fully infused with the energy you intend, and once it is cooled down enough to drink, enjoy.

Love Potion Tea and Incantation

- Chocolate Pu'er, damiana, dried strawberries, rosebuds, mint

"Waters of desire and passion, let romance grow. Open heart and open mind. The path of love will show from within and above. Waters flowing through me, bring me love."

Prosperi-Tea and Incantation

- Vanilla bean, cloves, dried apples, cinnamon, honey, yerba maté

"Belly full of laughs, plate full of glee. Glass full of vino, come drink with me. There's plenty for the taking, even more for creating my house full of riches, my heart full of tea."

Movement and Yoga Sequence for the Sacral

Balancing your sacral chakra is not just about shadow work and magical practices. Just like the root, we need to take back our belief and faith in ourselves, and we need to work to break up emotional blocks being held in the body with a physical release. I already mentioned dancing and using water for emotional release in the sacral, but the following is a yoga sequence that specifically targets the sacral.

1. **Sun Salutation (Surya Namaskar):**
   - Start in mountain pose (tadasana) with your feet together and palms at your heart center.
   - Inhale, raise your arms overhead, and gently arch back (upward salute/urdhva hastasana).

- Exhale, fold forward from your hips (forward fold / uttanasana), bending your knees if needed.
- Inhale, lengthen your spine, and lift your chest halfway (halfway lift / ardha uttanasana).
- Exhale, step or jump back into plank pose, aligning your wrists under your shoulders.
- Lower your body halfway down with bent elbows (chaturanga dandasana).
- Inhale, lift your chest, and gaze upward, coming into upward-facing dog (urdhva mukha svanasana).
- Exhale, lift your hips, and press back into downward-facing dog (adho mukha svanasana).
- Hold for a few breaths, then step or jump your feet between your hands.
- Inhale, lift your chest halfway (halfway lift / ardha uttanasana).
- Exhale, fold forward (forward fold / uttanasana).
- Inhale, sweep your arms out to the sides, and come up, reaching overhead (upward salute / urdhva hastasana).
- Exhale, bring your palms together at your heart center (mountain pose / tadasana).

2. **Crescent Pose (Anjaneyasana):**
   - From mountain pose, step your right foot back into a lunge position.
   - Lower your right knee to the ground and keep your left knee directly over your ankle.
   - Inhale, lift your torso, and raise your arms overhead.

- Sink into the lunge, keeping your core engaged and your shoulders relaxed.
- Gently tilt your head back or keep it neutral.
- Hold the pose for a few breaths, then repeat on the other side.

3. **Revolved Triangle (Parivrtta Trikonasana):**
   - From crescent pose, step your left foot back, turning it out to a 45-degree angle.
   - Square your hips toward the front of the mat.
   - Inhale, extend your arms out to the sides at shoulder height.
   - Exhale, hinge forward from your hips and reach your right hand down to the outside of your left foot.
   - Extend your left arm up toward the ceiling, creating a twist.
   - Gaze at your left hand or downward, whichever is comfortable.
   - Hold the pose for a few breaths, then repeat on the other side.

4. **Goddess Pose (Utkata Konasana):**
   - Stand with your feet wider than hip-width apart, toes turned out slightly.
   - Inhale, bend your knees, and sink into a wide-legged squat.
   - Exhale, bring your palms together at your heart center, pressing your elbows against your inner thighs.
   - Keep your chest lifted, shoulders relaxed, and core engaged.

- Hold the pose for a few breaths, feeling grounded and strong.

5. **Sun Salutation (Surya Namaskar):**
   - Repeat the Sun Salutation sequence described in step 1.

6. **Child's Pose (Balasana):**
   - Kneel on the floor, bringing your big toes together and sitting back on your heels.
   - Exhale, fold your torso forward, and rest your forehead on the mat.
   - Extend your arms forward or relax them by your sides.
   - Allow your body to relax completely and focus on deep, calming breaths.

7. **Corpse Pose (Savasana):**
   - Lie flat on your back with your legs extended and arms by your sides.
   - Close your eyes and let go of any tension in your body.
   - Relax your entire body and surrender to the pose.
   - Stay in this pose for a few minutes, focusing on relaxation and deep rest.

Remember to listen to your body and modify the poses as needed. If you're new to yoga or have any specific concerns, it's a good idea to seek guidance from a qualified yoga instructor. Enjoy your practice!

Meditations

Always start with the steps in the centering and grounding meditation that was described in the root chakra section of this book. You should become very familiar with this visualization. Think of this as the foundation to every meditation you do. You can always go to the rose garden as well in your meditations. The rose garden is meant to be a place of self-discovery—a place you can go to and discover where you may be on life's journey and practice with each chakra. I have used the space to clear out emotions and process events.

If you want to use the rose garden to receive messages specifically for the sacral chakra, make a mental note that you will be calling in the energy of the west, emotions, and water. You can also use the sacred circle if you built one and sit in the west section. However, there is an additional visualization for clearing, healing, and balancing the sacral.

The Healing Pond

You can do this in a bathtub with jasmine petals and incense or any combination of herbs and oils that are listed above. You can use music in the key of D as well to enhance the experience. However, you do not need any of this.

Whether in a body of water or simply in a comfortable sitting or reclining position, close your eyes and start to visualize the centering and grounding meditation, allowing the energy to travel through each chakra and then up around the aura as described in chapter two. Once the energy is activated (this first step takes practice; I would suggest doing this part alone every day), you will begin to feel light as your physical body stays in healing and your astral body again travels to your personal sanctuary.

The more you visit the sanctuary, the more you will notice. You may see representations of beliefs and journeys your soul has been on. You will also start to notice the many doors within the sanctuary. There is a fireplace and a bookshelf. For this meditation, you will see a door to the right of the fireplace. Take a moment to observe that door; there may be a guardian standing before it. Walk up and listen; often, there is a message before the door opens. Once you have paused to greet your guardian, the door will likely open.

On the other side of the door is a beautiful forest with tall redwood trees, a beautiful display of reds and greens. As you step into the forest, you may be able to feel the soil beneath your feet. It feels like silk and is filled with all the nourishing properties your body needs. You will notice there is a path of this rich, velvety soil to walk down. I like to take my time to observe any animals or lights within the forest that may appear.

Soon you will begin to hear the soft sound of running water, and as you do, you will notice an opening within the trees. In that opening is a small footbridge that passes over a flowing stream. The water within this stream is the clearest water you've ever seen. You can smell the fresh and calming water as you get closer. Once you have walked over the bridge, you will see a clearing, and in that clearing is a small pond just big enough to hold your body. There are beautiful slate stones that create the natural pond and vibrating crystals placed around the entire body of water. There is a small waterfall that keeps the water moving and refreshes the healing. You will submerge your astral body into the water. It is warm and soothing. Allow any emotions or thoughts that surface to flow freely as they are being washed away.

Allow yourself at least fifteen to twenty minutes to just soak. During this time, you may hear messages or be joined by spirit guides. Just allow them to be there. They are helpers of healing. You do not have to remember what is said to you, but if you do, you may want to write down the messages after the meditation to look at later.

Once you feel the energy start to fade and you are ready to come out of the meditation, you will step out of the water and visualize yourself going back over the bridge and through the woods. You will go back to your sanctuary and find the couch, allowing the visions of the room to dissipate and only seeing yourself surrounded by white light. Start to feel your physical body back in the room where you began the mediation. Feel your body from your toes to your head and every part in between. You will notice you feel heavy, present, and maybe a little dense again. At this point, you may open your eyes. This is important for closing the energy and becoming grounded and present. After each meditation, you should drink water and eat to ensure a grounded, stable presence.

The Sacral Activation

This one is a moving meditation and a very powerful ritual that can be used as spellwork. You can do this while walking (I like to do it on a treadmill so I don't fall), or it is most potent while dancing. Start with the centering and grounding visualization first mentioned in the root chakra, activating your chakras and psychic center. Yes, you can do this while moving. I close my eyes and either hold the sides of the treadmill or dance in an empty space where I won't hit anything.

Put on music that inspires you. This is not key specific; it's mostly music that gets you fired up and motivated, music that makes you happy. Whether walking or dancing, the movement and the music must be aligned to you and make you feel good.

You are not going on a visual journey this time. This meditation is about an emotional journey. You are not specifically focusing on release; that will come naturally. Instead, you are focusing on what you want to manifest or create in your life.

As you move and dance, you are going to visualize everything you desire, every detail of what it looks like, sounds like, smells like, feels like, and moves like. For example, if you want to change your physical appearance, see your body naked, from your toes to your head. Where are the muscles? How does the blood flow? See strong bones and organs. Visualize what your hair looks like, your face, and any other aesthetic you want to create. Maybe a body full of tattoos? Then see the external layer of clothing. What does it look like when you are most comfortable? Can you smell your scent? I always smell jasmine. What is your body physically capable of doing: running, jumping, pull-ups? Can you see yourself reaching new physical accomplishments? See all of this while you are moving.

These are just examples of what you may want to manifest and the details you want to see. It can be wealth, love, art, a house—it doesn't matter; just keep going and keep seeing it happen in detail. Your movement is allowing you to create a vibration and belief. Of course, this is also a form of sexual magic. You are using your body to become the creator.

Rituals

The rituals for the sacral chakra are all about creating your life, becoming the architect of your life, and building upon your new foundation. The first ritual is all about creating flow in your life and moving with fluidity. The second one is painting your heart's desires.

Alchemic Waters

For this ritual, you want to gather a few glass jars, usually Mason jars with lids. You will be working with water from any source you desire. Using water powered by the moon or other weather events is great when thinking about working with the sacral, your emotions, and the flow of creativity. The water is going to soak up the energy of whatever properties are at work. There are many books you can find that go in depth about moon water—what time of the year, what sign the moon is in, what phase, and so on. However, there isn't much written about things like using hurricane water or river water. Rule of thumb: every type of water is going to embody the energy of the words you would use to describe it. For example, a hurricane might be described as destructive and chaotic; therefore, using hurricane water will be invoking destructive, chaotic energy. You would use this energy when you are trying to break down your walls and create radical change.

After the jars are filled, speak a few sentences of energy into them. For example: "I will flow into a life of joy and abundance." I will also write these same words down on paper and tape them to the water jars. I do three jars: one for body, one for mind, and one for soul. I tape the paper with written words onto the jar of moon water, hurricane water, or whatever it may be. Then I read the piece of paper to the water every day and night for at least three days.

Painting

Painting is a creative form of water energy. You use the paint to dance around the canvas, aligning to the flow of energy that you want to create in your life. Now, this may be a little confusing because when I talk about manifesting, I literally tell my clients not to paint a picture of what it looks like, and I still mean that. I am not talking about creating a Thomas Kinkade painting. I am talking about painting with energy and emotion. More of a Jackson Pollock. When I'm doing this, I specifically paint hearts.

The first thing to do is get glue that dries clear but can leave a texture behind. I've tried glue guns, but they peel off the canvas too easily. I prefer to use white school glue (not glue sticks), the kind that squeezes out of a plastic bottle and is easy to write words with.

I do this ritual a lot. I do it during full moon energy, new moon energy, birthday, or any celestial event that carries a lot of manifesting energy. A rule of thumb I use when doing any ritual is to do it over three days: the day before, the day of, and the day after. This is a good one for that because after you write your words you will need to let the glue dry for twenty-four hours.

On the first day, you will start writing what you want to bring into your life on the canvas with the glue: happy, healthy romance; financial abundance; youthful, healthy body … whatever you want. The next day, you will use your paint colors. You can use any color palette. I suggest colors that make you feel the most like you (your favorite colors or color combinations). This is the best part: you are going to dip your fingertips into the paint and start drawing whatever you want. If you are feeling blocked with this, finger paint lines of hearts. Just keep going, making as many layers as you can. Put on your favorite music and your oldest clothes and get down and dirty with it. This is the day you just go to town. You will let that dry overnight, and on day three, with the lightest color paint you have been working with, you will make just a few lines or hearts on top of the fun you created yesterday. By adding this last layer with light-colored paint, you will be adding some depth, which will create a finished look.

When it's all done, it will be joyful, colorful, and oozing with happiness. The words you wrote first will appear as bumps under the layers of paint. You then have a painting you can hang or use as an altar item. Seeing it every day will allow it to become a living and breathing piece of energy.

Psychic Center of the Sacral

The sacral superpower is all about physical touch. When you combine your energy with another through touch, you can accelerate the rate of your healing or anything else you want to shift. However, there are other tools you can use to access this. Listening to your body, movement, being in the flow, imagery, and energetic imprints are all examples of how to gain access to the sacral superpower. Clairtangency is the ability to receive information with touch.

Psychometry

All living things leave energetic impressions. Sometimes those energetic memories become attached to articles of clothing, jewelry, plates, dishes—objects that have been used in routine over long periods of time. Sometimes those energetic memories simply live within an environment. For example, I am currently writing from an old house in Georgia that a friend of mine purchased a little less than two years ago. I know that he doesn't have any pets because he travels often for his career, but I keep seeing a dog and a cat in the house sitting on chairs, laying on the couch, etc. So I finally asked him, "Did the family that lived here before have one dog and one cat?" And he said yes. I told him I can see their energy all over the house. They are not ghosts. As you practice and get more familiar with the differences between energies, you'll be able to feel what is an energetic imprint or memory and what is an entity around you. The main difference is that ghosts may interact with you. They act as if they are presently in the situation. However, they are only memories and will have no interaction with you. You may see them interact with other energetic imprints from that time, but they don't act as if they are in the current reality.

Psychometry is when you begin to read the memories off an object. This was one of the first psychic abilities I learned. During my mother's Tuesday night meditation circles (we did not call them coven meetings at the time, too taboo), attendees would often bring old jewelry and heirlooms, and we would exchange the pieces, trying to read the energy from the object. Holding the object, I would close my eyes and start to see images in the form of a story.

I suggest you practice this as often as you can. Sometimes I tell clients to go shopping at antique shops where the shop owners may know the stories behind each object or to practice with friends who may have old jewelry or heirlooms with history and a story. Of course, do not tell each other the story, simply hold the object and begin sharing out loud whatever comes to mind. In the beginning it may be hard to trust that what is entering your mind is true energy and not your imagination, but the more you practice, the more you will feel the difference between energetic memories and imagination. It happens like this for me: when my imagination wants to put an image or a story to the energy embedded in the object, it won't stick. It pops like a thought bubble. It's almost as if the spirit is saying, "No, no, that doesn't belong here; cut it out."

The more you practice, the more you will feel the difference and the more you will trust the images that are coming to your mind. In the most recent psychometry session I did for someone, she brought me a small, cylindrical, metal bead-type object and told me absolutely nothing of its origin or history. I held the object and began getting images. I have lately developed this new way of seeing history. Spirit starts with me as if I am above the earth, and then I begin to drop somewhere.

On this particular day, I began to drop in somewhere in Far East Asia. I thought maybe Mongolia. I just spoke out loud as each image surfaced. I did not second guess what was coming or even really think about it. It became a flow of words strung together. First, I saw the feet of the person I seemed to be walking next to. I could feel his disposition; he was happy. I could see that he was greeting people in what looked like a market. Finally, I saw that he had a basket in his hands and that it was late morning. I could also see that he was wearing loose and light-fitting clothes but dark in color, almost like a deep purple. I could see he had some kind of cloth wrap around his waist. I just kept describing everything I was seeing as I was seeing it and everything I was feeling as I felt it. Oftentimes, spirit pauses the image until I say key descriptions, feelings, or words. This man continued walking for a while until it became late afternoon, and I felt his emotion change the closer he got to his home. Then, suddenly, I could hear his mind chatter, and for some reason I knew that he had no family even though people in town believed he did. His emotions went from pleasant and friendly to sad and lonely. Then as quickly as it started, it ended. The images just stopped coming. The feelings were turned off.

I opened my eyes and looked at the woman who had brought in this object and said, "That's all I could get." She then proceeded to tell me that she bought the object in an antique shop in Japan and the object was a belt adornment men used to wear. Nothing that I saw from the small bead indicated an origin, and I was not expecting such a story. To be honest, after more than thirty years of this, I still get amazed each time I do it.

This is a great place to start when you are learning to trust your psychic abilities. You will get immediate confirmation from the person who has brought the object to you if they know its history and origin. You will be able to practice your psychic vision (clairvoyance), psychic sense of emotions (clairsentience), possibly psychic knowing (claircognizant), and psychic smelling (clairalience).

Chapter Four
Solar Plexus Chakra, Manipura

Located slightly above the navel or a few inches below the sternum, the energy of the solar plexus deals with self-esteem, self-worth, physical energy, and social roles. This energy center is where we find our confidence without ego. A healthy solar plexus energy will show up as an individual who has balance within their life. For example, someone who knows when to work and when to play, who gives equal amounts of attention to their personal and professional lives. A healthy solar plexus also shows up in people who have and express healthy boundaries.

Both the solar plexus and the sacral are your generators. When in balance, you see yourself as being capable of anything. You can see the world as an opportunity instead of a burden. You can create the life you want from your sacral, but your solar plexus is where you put your limits or lack of limits. How you see yourself, how you show up, how you value yourself is all stored in the solar plexus. So now that you've created a healthy new foundation in the root and gained the trust in yourself in the sacral, how high can you go?

When I was heavily working within my solar plexus, I created an alter ego with a logo and everything. Her name is Lady Limitless, and the logo was an infinity symbol as an eye mask. Working to balance the solar plexus will give you the energy and motivation to go big. You will be able to express this energy in a sustainable way because you have a good work-home life balance, creating routines that nurture your body, mind, and soul.

The identity of the solar plexus, like the sacral chakra, also starts to develop in school-age years—primary and secondary through university. Sometimes we hear words of encouragement: "You can be anything you want." Too often we hear "That's not practical" or "That's a pipe dream," so we do something safe and secure, and we often squash our dreams and make ourselves much smaller than we can be.

My daughter is currently deciding her major in college, and she is thinking about going to nursing school. When I asked her why she thought about that as a career path and not the MBA she had always talked about, it sounded as if she was taking the "safe" solution. The safe solution works sometimes when we are unclear of what we want. I took a lot of safe roads as well as unsafe roads, but it all led to the same place. While I always knew I wanted to be a writer, without the detours in my life, I wouldn't have material to write about. Don't fear your decisions; they will always get you where you need to go.

I Do

The solar plexus chakra is our personal power, self-esteem, self-confidence, and the ability to take action. The affirmation "I do" reflects the proactive and assertive qualities associated with this chakra. This is where you get phrases like "Put your money where your mouth is" or "Actions are greater than words." When you are in alignment, you will do the things you say you will do. You will reach for the stars. You will go beyond your potential. You will take action toward your own joy and happiness.

Tools and Properties
of the Solar Plexus for Alignment

Emotional connections: Personal power center, sense of self, self-actualization, opinions, intellect, ambition, strength, courage, physical energy, will, and action

Physical connections: Stomach, liver, small intestines, pancreas, gall-bladder, waist

Foods: Lemons, bananas, pineapple, corn, squash, turmeric, ginger

Activities: Jumping, dancing, breath work

Color: Yellow—The solar plexus responds to yellow color therapy and balances when fed yellow foods.

Element: Fire—When you are feeling anxious, lighting a candle or sitting before a fire will calm that fire core and create a soothing energy within your solar plexus.

Tones and notes: E, aw—Listening to music, sounds, and frequencies that have these in them can break up blocks and clear out energy in the solar plexus. Chanting the sound "aw" is a very effective sound healing practice as well as listening to this chant. Sounds can be a very healing tool for anyone to use. Attend a sound healing class or listen to frequencies on any music app.

Gemstones

Gemstones have many uses for healing and vibrational alignment. They are widely used in holistic practices among many cultures. If you choose to work on one chakra at a time the way this book is laid out, you may want to wear gemstones as jewelry to create a vibrational frequency that aligns to the energy you are moving through. However, you can use them during meditation either on an altar or placed upon the chakra you are working with. You may want to set a routine for this type of meditation or for when you are in the middle of experiencing the emotions. Setting multiple gemstones together around the house in a patterned grid amplifies the energy you are working with and creates movement of this energy. You can do this during the entire cycle of working with this chakra, then change the grid when you move to the next chakra.

Topaz: This stone improves decision-making abilities and promotes a sense of mental stability. Topaz's energy can help individuals gain a clearer perspective and find clarity in their thoughts and actions. Topaz amplifies intentions, enhances manifestation practices, and attracts prosperity and success. Topaz's energy can support individuals in manifesting their goals and desires, fostering a positive and abundant mindset. It promotes self-expression, enhances leadership qualities, and encourages assertiveness. Topaz's energy can help individuals embrace their personal power, speak their truth, and stand tall in their authentic selves. Topaz uplifts the spirit, promotes a positive outlook, and infuses life with happiness. Its energy can help individuals cultivate a sense of joy, gratitude, and enthusiasm, fostering a vibrant and optimistic approach to life.

Citrine: This stone attracts wealth, prosperity, and success. Citrine's energy is thought to assist in setting intentions, amplifying positive energy, and attracting opportunities for financial abundance and material well-being. Citrine helps alleviate depression, enhance self-confidence, and foster a positive outlook on life. Citrine clears stagnant or negative energies from the aura and the environment, promoting energetic renewal and a sense of vitality. Citrine's energy can assist in removing energetic blockages and creating a harmonious and uplifting atmosphere. Citrine stimulates and activates this chakra, enhancing personal power, confidence, and self-expression. Citrine's energy can support a balanced and empowered sense of self, promoting courage and motivation.

Yellow tiger's eye: This stone's energy can help anchor and stabilize one's energy field, providing a sense of security and protection. Yellow tiger's eye stimulates the solar plexus chakra, promoting self-confidence, motivation, and assertiveness. Its energy can assist in overcoming self-doubt, fears, and challenges, allowing individuals to step into their personal power and embrace their true potential. Yellow tiger's eye enhances decision-making abilities. It can help clear mental fog, improve concentration, and facilitate strategic thinking. It helps bring about a sense of balance between masculine and feminine aspects, promoting harmony and wholeness. This stone's energy can support the integration and alignment of different aspects of one's personality. Yellow tiger's eye assists individuals in embracing spiritual transformation. Yellow tiger's eye helps manifest financial stability, success, and opportunities. Its energy can support a positive mindset, attract abundance, and assist in achieving financial goals.

Yellow jasper: This stone helps individuals embrace their personal power, overcome self-doubt, and stand in their authentic selves. Yellow jasper's energy can support individuals in asserting themselves and expressing their true potential. Yellow jasper assists in manifesting one's intentions and attracting prosperity, wealth, and success. Its energy can help individuals focus their energy and manifest their desires in alignment with their highest good. Yellow jasper is known for its calming and stabilizing properties. It is believed to provide emotional support, promote inner strength, and aid in emotional healing. Yellow jasper's energy can help individuals release negative emotions, reduce stress, and restore emotional balance. It stimulates and balances this chakra, promoting personal power and confidence. Yellow jasper's energy can help individuals align with their purpose, boost their creativity. This stone is often linked to optimism, joy, and positive thinking. It uplifts the spirit, brings a sense of enthusiasm, and promotes a positive outlook on life.

Oils and Herbs

As with gemstones, oils and herbs can be used in many ways during the healing process. I like to use these specifically during difficult times while working through each energy field. Not only can you experience moments of intense emotion, you may also experience what's called a healing crisis. Sometimes during a healing crisis it can feel like you have flu-like symptoms. This is actually the toxins leaving the body. You can experience this after a reiki session or sometimes after a yoga sequence. There are other times you may experience a healing crisis, and in these instances, I find it useful to use the oils and herbs. This is also a good time to drink the tea blends.

> *Ginger:* Thought to awaken the senses, boost vitality, and provide a sense of renewed energy, ginger's energy can be used to overcome lethargy, promote motivation, and stimulate the flow of life force energy in the body. Ginger is used to ease digestive discomfort and support healthy

digestion. In a spiritual context, ginger is believed to help process and assimilate emotions, thoughts, and experiences. It can be used to facilitate the release and transformation of emotional blockages or stagnation.

Saffron: This spice is associated with the integration of physical, mental, and spiritual aspects of life. Saffron's energetic properties can help restore equilibrium, promote emotional well-being, and foster a sense of inner peace. Saffron is associated with the sun, and fire represents the transformative power of light and enlightenment. Saffron's energy can support individuals in their spiritual journeys, facilitating personal growth and expanding consciousness.

Geranium: This plant helps alleviate stress and anxiety and promotes emotional well-being. Geranium is often used to restore emotional balance and foster a sense of inner peace. Geranium encourages self-acceptance, nurtures inner beauty, and fosters a positive self-image. It can be used to cultivate a sense of self-worth and enhance feelings of love and compassion toward oneself. Geranium supports the release of emotional wounds and facilitates inner growth and transformation. Geranium can be used in rituals or practices aimed at healing and letting go of past traumas or emotional blockages. Geranium invigorates the senses, promotes positive thinking, and enhances vitality. Its uplifting properties can be used to overcome lethargy, boost mood, and inspire a sense of joy and optimism.

Rosemary: This herb creates a shield against negative energies, wards off evil spirits, and purifies the energy of a space. Rosemary can be used to clear away stagnant or heavy energies, creating a sacred and harmonious environment. Rosemary supports physical and emotional healing processes. It can be used to promote vitality, strengthen the immune system, and provide a sense of renewal and rejuvenation.

Clary sage: This herb can be used to cleanse and protect the aura, establish boundaries, and maintain a sacred and protected space. Clary sage alleviates stress, anxiety, and emotional tension. Its energy can support emotional healing, release emotional blockages, and foster a sense of inner peace and tranquility.

Shadow Work

1. Where are your physical issues? If you have stomach issues, maybe start with the solar plexus. If you are not sure about what is physically out of alignment, I would simply start with the root and move up from there.

2. Once you decide which chakra you are going to start focusing on, put your energy and thoughts toward that chakra at night. Even before knowing what may come up, simply put your hands on that energy center as you fall asleep. You can send healing light visually to that chakra and say out loud or to yourself "I am ready to release any stuck and unhealed energy. I am ready to see what has been hiding in the shadows." Then be open to what happens next. Your days to follow will bring up issues you have been avoiding.

3. Set time aside weekly for processing the emotions, emotional reactions, triggers, and social interactions

that are coming up. You may even want to do this daily before you go to bed. Start journaling the questions you are asking and answering for yourself.

4. Finally, decide which of the provided tools you will use and create a routine for each. Slowly integrate changes into your routine. Do not try to do everything all at once. In order to create sustainable lifestyle changes, you should start with one at a time. After you feel comfortable with steps two and three, maybe add drinking herbal teas or yoga once a week.

Questions for Solar Plexus Chakra Shadow Work

How do you demonstrate your commitment to your ideas and passions when sharing them with others? How do you balance sharing past experiences with showcasing your current abilities and pursuing new ideas or adventures? How would you describe your approach to moving forward and executing new solutions in your life? How do you perceive the patterns in your life, and what steps do you take to break free from repeating past mistakes? When you talk, listen to how long ago those actions took place.

So many times in society, we hold onto moments in the past when we were living our "glory" days. We have been conditioned to believe there comes a time in life when we have to settle down or act our age. Time becomes the enemy of "I do." We believe we must have certain things accomplished by certain ages. Releasing this notion of age and time frees you up to "do" anything you want at any time you're ready.

When working with the solar plexus, one of the first things we have to overcome is our idea of time—our idea that life has to be lived one step at a time in consecutive order. This belief that you're too late creates paralysis. We have to give up the idea of time. Just because you have been doing something for six months doesn't mean you should have already accomplished whatever it is you are working toward. After you realize time has nothing to do with the destination—that it's only about the journey—you then have to realize that the journey is the only true path to getting there.

Ask yourself: What do you do to get yourself out of a funk? Your daily routines are important to keep you moving forward. Every successful person has a lifestyle where they begin with the end in mind, then create the path they will follow.

Once you get to your personal starting point, start with no excuses. However, what about the days when those excuses are really loud? What strategies do you employ on days you just can't seem to get into the routine?

While taking action, it is important to honor your moment and listen to the pace that is right. You want to make sure you are always mindful of your emotions and not just "powering through." Suppressed or ignored emotions will always lead to bigger issues. Even on your healing journey it is unrealistic to think you have to be light and love constantly. Sometimes I want to listen to Adele and other times I want to listen to Five Finger Death Punch. I pay attention to what is going to boost my mood and not hinder it, and sometimes it is as simple as knowing what you want in the moment you want it.

However, this can also have negative effects if your coping methods are impulsiveness or acting out. The solar plexus is where the addictions will take hold. In the sacral is where the void is created, but the action we take to fill the void is in the solar plexus. Remember, the solar plexus is "I do," so what are you doing to balance this energy?

On low-energy days, I make sure I do the laundry. I don't have to watch the clothes spin; I just have to put them in, then go back to vegging out. It is important to me to have a clean house, so this is a great strategy for low-energy days. And on low-emotion days, I watch comedies. Even if I don't get out of bed and happen to put on a tearjerker or two, I will always make sure I put on at least one stand-up routine to make sure I don't slide completely down the rabbit hole.

When I really started my healing journey at the age of forty, I had no idea how young I was going to get and how much more I was going to do. I had a good career in education. I had acquired tons of degrees, had kids, and was now divorced. What was there to look forward to? What more was my life going to do? Little did I know I was going to retire from education and start a whole new career. I started dating millennials. That wasn't the intention going into it, but it was the energy and the conversations I was drawn to. I started going to music festivals; a lot of times I was the oldest in the room but not always. Then you read about people like Vera Wang, who didn't create her first dress until her forties.

The most important thing I have learned to do for myself through my healing journey and studies is to make sure I am honoring my emotions and energy level. Just like most people, and maybe even more so, I would get really down on myself if I missed a day of work or a deadline. I felt guilty for being sick, which always made me sicker. Now I listen to all parts of my body, and if one of them says slow down, I slow down. If they say full speed ahead, I go full speed ahead. I make plans for myself and with others that I am not afraid to break if my body has made other plans.

Letter for Solar Plexus Chakra Shadow Work

During the full moon, the light is at its brightest, and immediately after that, it begins to lose its glow. This is why we use the full moon to release energy. You are viewing the full moon as the starting point. The new moon lacks all light, but the very next day it begins to gain its light and brilliance. You want to think of this as a complete cycle for transformation. The solar plexus is where you want to create new habits of action—things you can do that cause productivity in your life.

If you have addictions you need to let go of, start at the full moon and write your thirty-day intention. Keep it simple at first until you start to see some progress in old habits being released and new, healthy habits coming in. Here's an example:

> *Tonight I am releasing my urge to drink as a way to relax my mind and body. I am ready for a new, healthy way to relax that will promote a feeling of motivation and vigor in the morning.*

Letters to Write to Yourself When Healing the Solar Plexus

What are my unhealthy behaviors and actions that leave me feeling unaccomplished toward my goals?

> *Dear Stefani, no longer will you allow your feelings of loneliness and fear to dictate your actions. You have come far and know with faith in your heart that acting on the impulses that are driven by fear will only derail your future of joy and happiness. You will act when your body, mind, and soul all scream yes! This is the right way. You know when you can trust those energies and when they show up as a trauma response. You have the full power to only choose actions that will increase your health, wealth, and sexual-*

ity. Keep making those moves toward your biggest dreams. You are constantly arriving at a better place.

Affirmations for Solar Plexus Chakra Energy Work

I take charge and seize the day in alignment to my highest good!
I do whatever it takes to stay motivated, strong, and courageous
to push forward in life, making new waves every day!

Recipes for Solar Plexus Chakra Energy Work

For each tea blend, I use loose-leaf herbs and tea leaves and make the blends in 20-ounce Mason jars. I use equal parts of each ingredient, and I have listed about ⅓ of a cup for each ingredient. I gently roll the Mason jar to mix the ingredients together without breaking up the herbs into dust.

When I'm ready to brew the tea, I heat up water in a teapot and scoop a tablespoon of the blend into a reusable tea bag. I then add my tea bag plus other ingredients such as honey or lemon (to taste) to a mug before the water is done. When the water is hot, I add it to the mug slowly.

To activate the tea with the incantation, I do a few things: First, I will write the incantation onto a sticky note and put it on the pot as it heats the water. As I pour the water slowly, I will read the incantation out loud. I stop the pour with enough room at the top of my mug so that the next part does not cause the water to spill out. Once the water is a little cooled down, I will place my right hand over the top of the mug and grasp it (not by its handle but by the rim) so that the energy from my hand is also infused into the water. Once I have a firm grip, I will pick it up and swirl the mug and tea clockwise three times while saying the incantation. I will also repeat this on my left side three times but counterclockwise. Then I will go back to my right hand and repeat the swirl but counterclockwise then right hand clockwise.

Your tea is now fully infused with the energy you intend, and once it is cooled down enough to drink, enjoy.

Waking the Beast Tea and Incantation

- Ginger, lemon, cayenne, yerba maté, new moon water, damiana

"Starting new, so much to do. Ignite the passion, turn on the flame. The warrior is coming to slay the game."

Turning Up the Heat Tea and Incantation

- Dandelion, lemon, yerba maté, echinacea, yarrow, full moon water

"Out with the old, stagnant, and stuck. In with the gold replacing the muck. Clearing the path, finding the way. Time for the sun to shine on today."

Movement and Yoga Sequence for the Solar Plexus

Balancing your solar plexus chakra can change your energy levels and bring adventure back into your life. It may cause you to feel a bit more extroverted and take risks. It may also cause confidence and strength. Opening and balancing the solar plexus will make you feel freer. Move your body, jump, dance, take a breath work class, and feel the fire ignite.

1. **Sun Salutation (Surya Namaskar):**
   - Start in mountain pose (tadasana) with your feet together and palms at your heart center.

- Inhale, raise your arms overhead, and gently arch back (upward salute / urdhva hastasana).
- Exhale, fold forward from your hips (forward fold / uttanasana), bending your knees if needed.
- Inhale, lengthen your spine, and lift your chest halfway (halfway lift / ardha uttanasana).
- Exhale, step or jump back into plank pose, aligning your wrists under your shoulders.
- Lower your body halfway down with bent elbows (chaturanga dandasana).
- Inhale, lift your chest, and gaze upward, coming into upward-facing dog (urdhva mukha svanasana).
- Exhale, lift your hips, and press back into downward-facing dog (adho mukha svanasana).
- Hold for a few breaths, then step or jump your feet between your hands.
- Inhale, lift your chest halfway (halfway lift / ardha uttanasana).
- Exhale, fold forward (forward fold / uttanasana).
- Inhale, sweep your arms out to the sides, and come up, reaching overhead (upward salute / urdhva hastasana).
- Exhale, bring your palms together at your heart center (mountain pose / tadasana).

2. **Bow Pose (Dhanurasana):**
- Lie flat on your stomach with your arms by your sides.

- Bend your knees and reach back to hold onto your ankles or feet.
- Inhale, lift your chest and thighs off the mat, arching your back.
- Keep your gaze forward or slightly upward.
- Press your feet into your hands, lifting your body higher.
- Hold the pose for a few breaths, feeling a gentle stretch in your front body.

3. **Sun Salutation (Surya Namaskar):**
   - Repeat the Sun Salutation sequence described in step 1.

4. **Crescent Pose (Anjaneyasana):**
   - From mountain pose, step your right foot back into a lunge position.
   - Lower your right knee to the ground and keep your left knee directly over your ankle.
   - Inhale, lift your torso, and raise your arms overhead.
   - Sink into the lunge, keeping your core engaged and your shoulders relaxed.
   - Gently tilt your head back or keep it neutral.
   - Hold the pose for a few breaths, then repeat on the other side.

5. **Sun Salutation (Surya Namaskar):**
   - Repeat the Sun Salutation sequence described in step 1.

6. **Camel Pose (Ustrasana):**
   - Kneel on the mat with your knees hip-width apart.

- Place your hands on your lower back, fingers pointing downward.
- Inhale, lift your chest and gently arch backward.
- Reach your hands toward your heels, one at a time.
- Keep your neck relaxed and gaze upward or slightly behind you.
- Hold the pose for a few breaths, feeling a deep opening in your chest and shoulders.

7. **Knees to Chest (Apanasana):**
   - Lie flat on your back with your legs extended.
   - Hug your knees into your chest and wrap your arms around them.
   - Gently rock side to side to massage your lower back.
   - Breathe deeply and release any tension in your body.

8. **Corpse Pose (Savasana):**
   - Release your knees and extend your legs flat on the mat.
   - Close your eyes and let go of any effort.
   - Relax your entire body, allowing it to sink into the ground.
   - Stay in this pose for several minutes, focusing on relaxation and stillness.

Remember to listen to your body and modify the poses as needed. If you're new to yoga or have any specific concerns, it's a good idea to seek guidance from a qualified yoga instructor. Enjoy your practice!

Meditations

The solar plexus meditations are all about you taking control of your life, taking back your power. Start with the centering and grounding meditation in the place you have designated and set up for meditation during the root chakra. By now, you will most likely have a good routine, and the energy should just start to flow. After you have gotten yourself centered, you will return to the sanctuary as you have done in the previous beginnings. From there we will go to the window found on the west wall of the sanctuary.

The Window

For this meditation you are going to learn to fly. This time in the sanctuary you will notice one of the walls is nothing but a huge window from floor to ceiling. However, as you look at the window, it is hard to see what is on the outside. You will notice a door in the center of the glass. Walk toward the door, and it will open for you. On the other side of the window is what looks like a wooded area. You will notice you are on a small hill, and you need to walk down toward a creek. It is easy to walk across by stepping on the stones that look as if nature intended to create the bridge for you. On the other side is a much bigger hill that you must climb. Notice this hill: Is it more like a mountain? Notice the level of difficulty you perceive this climb to be. You will make it to the top no matter what, so keep climbing.

Once you reach the top, you will notice that you can see an entire valley. How big that valley is and what is down there depends on your personal journey at the time of the meditation. This will change each time you visit over the years because your life is always moving forward.

You will be visited by spirit guides once you arrive. These guides will take many forms, and if you are visited by a form you don't recognize, you can look it up on the computer. Listen and feel the messages. You will then be prompted by your guides to jump. Have no fear; this is where you will build strength and courage to keep going. You will fly. You will see the valley below, and you will know anything is possible.

The Solar Plexus Activation

This is all about listening to your body and learning to trust the physical sensations you feel when faced with a decision or around a new person or situation. We all know that feeling of uneasiness or anxiety—that "gut feeling." Do we always listen and trust the gut feeling? How can we learn to always trust our body?

There are different voices running through your body that you will learn about later in the book. There are times it is good to listen to each of them. Once you become aware of how they sound and feel, you will begin to trust yourself. You will be able to identify a healthier response and behavior pattern.

After you practice this exercise and get reacquainted with your body, you will notice how often it truly does talk to us. That stomach cramp is telling you something. That twitch in your eye: Who is trying to deceive you? That bouncing knee isn't always nervousness: Where does it want to lead you? The itch on the palm of your hand: What's coming in for you? Your body will become a new language when you listen.

I first learned about using the body as a pendulum when I was learning what foods my body best responds to. Our body intuitively knows what's good for us and what's not. You need to stand straight and still. Try to calm the mind. If the chatter in the mind continues, just put it on the back burner like background music that we aren't paying attention to. Then you will ask the body, "Please show me yes" and allow your body to move on its own without a signal from your mind. You will notice a slight movement either forward, backward, or to one side. Once you do this, it's most likely that will always be your yes, but you can ask a few different times just to make sure your body is staying with the same directions. Calm your mind again after you get the direction for yes, then ask, "Which way is no?" Pay attention to which direction you are pulled in and remember this will most likely always be the case, but you can check more than once while you are learning.

Once you're comfortable with the different directions the body has shown you for yes and no, it's time to ask a few practice questions. You could use food to practice. For example: "Is dairy good for my body?" You could even be more specific about types of dairy. I would practice as much as possible to understand how the body works as a pendulum. Once you feel ready to tackle big questions, you can ask things like "Should I go on this date?" or "Should I take this job?" or "Should I release this person from my life?" or "Should I go on this trip?" Any yes or no question you can think of, you can use your body to intuitively tell you what you already know. This is a great way to build up your self-confidence when it comes to decision-making. Eventually you will be able to listen to your body without having to ask the question directly. Your body will just start talking to you because you have gained confidence in your body. This confidence in your body will create a great deal of strength and healing for you.

Ritual

The ritual for the solar plexus chakra is all about self-worth, strength, and courage. For this ritual you will be focused on taking back your power. The solar plexus is the fire energy in the body. You can think of it as the heat you generate when inspired.

Solar Flare

To harness the courage and strength of the solar plexus, I like using candles or a firepit. There are many ways to use candles in ritual work and many books that will explain how to use colors, sigils, and herbs. I am not going to break down all the ways you can practice with candles. I am going to share with you the one way I have used candles for the past forty years.

I use a white seven-day candle for all of my candle work. A seven-day candle is a candle in a tall glass cylinder and often has a saint on it. I use just white with no saint or deity associated with it. Every now and then for special occasions I will stray from my routine, but mostly it's always a white seven-day candle. The white candle brings in your higher consciousness, guardians, angels, or deities; it connects you to the higher realm. When I am calling for the fire in my spirit to be turned on or up, I call in my guides and protectors to walk this journey with me. I write my intentions on paper and tape that paper to the glass of the candle. You will also need a separate place, such as a firepit or firesafe bowl, at the end of this ritual to burn the paper you will be using to write your intention on.

I tend to be more direct and specific with what I want to attract with this work. This work also tends to have a very effective ripple of energy. You will be able to see this work affect all parties involved if you are doing work for more than just yourself. A fire ritual is one of the strongest you can work with. Fire is as destructive as it is cleansing. Be mindful of this while working with its energy. Be careful what you wish for.

Please be direct with what you want while working with fire to avoid getting burned, physically or emotionally. An example of words I have used are: "I am powerful, and my actions are always pushing me forward. I am full of ambition and will to sculpt my reality. The body I desire is what everyone sees, including me." This is about health and fitness but also adds the motivation for myself to do the work.

Relight the candle every day until it can no longer be lit. Read your statement every day while the candle is burning as often as possible whenever you see it. When the candle has completely burned down, you will burn the paper in the firepit and dispose of the glass. If you do not have a firepit, you can use a firesafe bowl to completely burn the paper.

Psychic Center of the Solar Plexus

The solar plexus is about learning to trust yourself. It's also a physical chakra like the sacral and the root, but here you want to learn to trust your own body and your own energy. The tool that fits the best to open the solar plexus superpowers is the pendulum.

Growing up, my mom loved to teach meditation, but the other two things we did often during her Tuesday night groups were psychometry, which I talked about with the sacral, and the pendulum. We would spend the first hour of the night exchanging items we wore and asking each other yes or no questions with the pendulum. To this day, I still use a pendulum. I currently have one that my mother made. It is a hand-twisted copper chain around an obsidian arrowhead that has a clear quartz and two small pieces of moldavite on it. I use the pendulum whenever I am unclear on the path I should choose. I also use it to open and balance the chakras when I am doing a healing session.

Pendulum

A pendulum can be a physical item, usually a weight at the end of a chain; however, you can also use your own body. When using an actual pendulum, you will start by asking it which way is yes and which way is no. Hold the top bead of your pendulum gently in your dominant hand and place your other hand flat under the point of the pendulum. Then ask your questions. Pause between each question. Sometimes the pendulum will spin in a direction that it did not indicate as yes or no. You can add, "Which way is maybe?" and "Which way is 'I don't know'?" I have found that these come up infrequently; however, they do come up. Practice with only your hand for some time before you incorporate a pendulum board. The reason I advise this is because you can influence the direction of the pendulum with your mind, and you want to train your mind to be completely still while asking questions. That is why this is one of the first techniques I like to teach in conjunction with listening to your body.

Learning how to quiet the ego so as not to influence the energy and learning to understand what your body is saying are essential when developing all other psychic abilities. Practice this as often as possible, at least once a day. You will know you are proficient in this when your doubt goes away and you fully trust the yes or no answers you are receiving. As you read on in this book, you will discover the different energies that speak to us.

Chapter Five
Heart Chakra, Anahata

Located at the center of the chest, this energy is the first of the "higher-level" chakras. The first three connect us to the earth and our assertive power energy. The heart is the beginning of the celestial connection and our nurturing energy. Here we start to let go of our human concerns and work more with compassion and unconditional love.

The intimacy of the heart chakra is a very different energy than the intimacy of the lower three, where we have to connect to our vulnerability. Here, our intimacy is with an open heart and the ability to love without expectation. When your heart is healed, you will be able to trust, love, and feel connected to all things. You will also be able to see yourself as one with all things while simultaneously knowing others' choices and actions have nothing to do with you.

The heart chakra is always looking to connect. Sometimes it reaches out for connection from a place of pain; sometimes it reaches out from a place of joy. Sometimes we need to receive a connection; other times we need to give it. The heart is always active no matter how much we think we are protecting it. The heart strength is ever present. The need we have in our heart chakra ebbs and flows. Sometimes we get stuck in an attachment for better or for worse. There is no distinction in the heart; it is just the strength of the energy and attachment.

There are many ways that our heart chakra becomes attached and forms a bond. It can form an identity that most people don't recognize as a heart chakra attachment. I had a client once ask me, "Why do I love going to church mass on Sundays? I am not Catholic." I told her, "Because everyone who attends mass or any church service has agreed to open their heart chakras while they are there. Each of them have energetically decided they are coming to give and receive unconditional love. It's the same when you go to any type of group recovery meeting. We are in agreement to support and share with open hearts." The answer was simple yet hidden from her awareness, and she immediately understood.

When a large number of people come together and agree to experience an open-heart chakra, the danger then becomes attachment and getting stuck to what the group has achieved. Some people chase that high. Just like any other drug, they will look to re-create the experience while they are not in the exchange. That's when you see people become preachers of the institution, whether it's a religious belief or a recovery system. It's hard for people to experience such an intense high and leave it in the next moment. However, if you can become unattached to the experience and just appreciate it for what it is in the moment, you will be able to train your energy to flow through all experiences easily. You will be able to let go of what doesn't serve you. You will be able to integrate what does. You will also be able to grieve without disturbing your happiness. This is the beginning of really allowing yourself to feel the flow.

Grief is one of the hardest emotions we process because we view it as losing a piece of our heart. A healed heart will remember we haven't lost anything. People may have left our world, our lives, or even our surroundings; your career or family may have changed. A healed heart can reflect on what that experience filled our heart with. We can start to look at our relationships with people, places, and things without attachment. Even our own existence is temporary, and we must not attach to any of it. Don't attach to the highs or lows.

I Love

The heart chakra is full of love, compassion, forgiveness, and the ability to connect with others. The affirmation "I love" reflects the loving and compassionate qualities of this chakra. It emphasizes the capacity to give and receive love, feel empathy, and cultivate a deep sense of compassion. Sometimes this is all we need to heal our entire journey—just to remember that we do love; we are love. When we truly feel love in our hearts, the world starts to look different. This is hard to find and experience. Real love comes without attachment. Real love just is. It generates from the heart, and there is no cap. It is limitless! I don't love my daughter 50 percent and my son 50 percent. I love them both 100 percent, and I can love as many people as I want with all of my heart. I don't have to piece it out, and the more I love without conditions, the more I feel love.

Tools and Properties of the Heart for Alignment

Emotional connections: Unconditional love for self and others, compassion, nurturing, healing, trust, empathy, connection, intuition, issues of worth, loneliness, receiving and giving, attachments, Christ love

Physical connections: Liver, stomach, heart, lungs, chest, breasts, pectoral muscles, hands, forearms, shoulders, rib cage, thymus gland, respiratory

Foods: Leafy greens, mint, cucumber, celery, avocado, brussels sprouts, green beans, kiwi, dragon fruit

Activities: Workouts that develop the arms and shoulders. Push-ups are very good for opening the heart.

Colors: Green and rose—The heart responds to green and pink vibrations. There is an etheric heart also. These are the pinks and whites we see when the heart is at its highest vibration.

Element: Air—Doing breath work is another healing technique for the heart. There are many different breath work techniques out there. When looking for breath work, do your research and listen to your body. Breath work can be a very intense release.

Tones and notes: F, ah—Listening to music, sounds, and frequencies that have these in them can break up blocks and clear out energy in the heart. Sounds can be a very healing tool for anyone to use. Attend a sound healing class or listen to frequencies on any music app. Chanting the "ah" sound is a very effective sound healing practice.

Gemstones

Gemstones have many uses for healing and vibrational alignment. They are widely used in holistic practices among many cultures. If you choose to work on one chakra at a time the way this book is laid out, you may want to wear gemstones as jewelry to create a vibrational frequency that aligns to the energy you are moving through. However, you can use them during meditation either on an altar or placed upon the chakra you are working with. You may want to set a routine for this type of meditation or for when you are in the middle of experiencing the emotions. Setting multiple gemstones together around the house in a patterned grid amplifies the energy you are working with and creates movement of this energy. You can do this during the entire cycle of working with this chakra, then change the grid when you move to the next chakra.

Jade: This stone attracts wealth, luck, and success. Jade's energy is said to create a harmonious flow of positive energy, promoting financial growth and opportunities. It is also believed to help in manifesting one's desires and bringing about prosperity in all areas of life. Jade promotes physical, emotional, and spiritual healing. Jade is often used to restore balance and harmony to the body, mind, and spirit. It is believed to support the overall health and vitality of an individual. Jade shields the wearer from negative energies, harm, and negative influences. Jade brings peace, tranquility, and a sense of emotional stability. Jade is often used to calm the mind, release stress, and promote inner peace. It is said to balance and align the energies of the body and spirit. Jade enhances intuition, insight, and spiritual awareness. Jade is often used in meditation and spiritual practices to gain clarity, guidance, and a deeper understanding of oneself and the world. Jade attracts love, deepens existing relationships, and promotes harmony in partnerships. Jade's energy is said to nurture love and compassion, fostering a sense of connection, understanding, and forgiveness.

Peridot: This stone has a rejuvenating effect on the body, mind, and spirit. Peridot is associated with promoting physical and emotional healing, releasing old patterns or attachments, and facilitating personal growth and transformation. Peridot opens the heart chakra, promoting love, compassion, and forgiveness. Peridot can help release emotional baggage, heal past wounds, and foster a sense of emotional well-being and inner harmony. Peridot enhances spiritual growth, intuition, and spiritual awareness. Peridot can assist in deepening one's connection to higher realms, receiving spiritual guidance, and expanding consciousness. Peridot uplifts the spirits, promotes a positive mindset, and inspires a sense of joy and enthusiasm for life. Peridot can help dispel negativity, alleviate stress, and enhance overall happiness.

Rose quartz: This stone opens and heals the heart, promoting self-love, compassion, and forgiveness. Rose quartz can help cultivate a deeper sense of love and acceptance toward oneself and others, fostering harmonious relationships and emotional healing. Rose quartz soothes emotional wounds, alleviates stress and anxiety, and restores emotional balance. Rose quartz can help release negative emotions, promote self-care, and create a sense of overall well-being. It activates and harmonizes the heart chakra, facilitating the flow of love and promoting a deeper connection with oneself and others. Rose quartz can help heal heart-related issues and support emotional and personal growth. This stone encourages self-exploration and self-awareness. It can assist in identifying and releasing emotional blockages, promoting inner healing and transformation. Rose quartz attracts and enhances romantic love, deepens existing relationships, and encourages understanding.

Green aventurine: This stone soothes emotional wounds, promotes emotional healing, and restores balance to the heart. Green aventurine can help release emotional blockages, foster self-love, and cultivate harmonious relationships. It supports personal growth, creativity, and vitality. Green aventurine can assist in overcoming challenges, embracing change, and discovering new opportunities for growth and expansion. It attracts fortunate circumstances, synchronicities, and positive experiences. Green aventurine can assist in being in the right place at the right time and recognizing opportunities that come along.

Watermelon tourmaline: This stone opens and activates the heart chakra, promoting love, compassion, and emotional healing. Watermelon tourmaline can help cultivate a deeper sense of love, acceptance, and forgiveness toward oneself and others. It combines the energies of both green and pink tourmaline, representing the harmonious integration of masculine and feminine energies. Its energy is said to promote balance between the mind, body, and spirit, fostering overall well-being and inner harmony. Watermelon tourmaline is associated with enhancing the flow of energy throughout the body. Its energy is believed to support vitality, stamina, and physical well-being. Watermelon tourmaline can help release stagnant energy, promote a healthy energy flow, and rejuvenate the body and mind. It is known for its vibrant and joyful energy. Its playful and uplifting vibrations boost mood, increase optimism, and inspire a sense of joy and lightheartedness. Watermelon tourmaline can assist in embracing the joy of life and finding delight in the present moment.

Emerald: This stone opens and activates the heart chakra, promoting unconditional love, empathy, and emotional healing. Emerald can help foster harmonious relationships, enhance the ability to give and receive love, and encourage forgiveness and understanding. Emerald is the stone of inspiration and infinite patience. It brings domestic bliss and loyalty. Known as the stone of successful love, it enhances unity, partnership, and friendship. Emerald supports overall well-being, strengthens the immune system, and aids in recovery from illness or injury. Emerald can also help restore balance and harmony to the mind, body, and spirit.

Rhodochrosite: This stone opens and activates the heart chakra, promoting self-love, forgiveness, and emotional healing. Rhodochrosite can help dissolve emotional blockages, release past wounds, and cultivate a deeper sense of love and empathy toward oneself and others. Rhodochrosite facilitates self-awareness, enhances self-esteem, and promotes personal transformation. Rhodochrosite can assist in uncovering and releasing negative patterns, supporting personal growth, and encouraging a positive self-image. It helps elevate mood, increases optimism, and inspires a sense of joy and enthusiasm for life. Rhodochrosite can assist in embracing the present moment, finding pleasure in simple joys, and cultivating a positive outlook.

Prehnite: This stone opens and activates the heart chakra, promoting love, compassion, and emotional balance. Prehnite can help release emotional wounds, alleviate stress and anxiety, and foster a sense of inner peace and harmony. Prehnite helps soothe the mind, release worries and fears, and promote a sense of tranquility. It is often used for meditation or relaxation practices, assisting in achieving a state of deep calmness and serenity. Prehnite is known for its gentle and uplifting energy. Its vibrations help increase optimism, and promote a positive outlook on life. Prehnite assists in cultivating a sense of serenity, enhancing self-confidence, and attracting positive experiences.

Malachite: This stone facilitates deep inner healing, personal growth, and spiritual evolution. Malachite assists in breaking through old patterns, releasing emotional traumas, and supporting positive change. Malachite is closely associated with the heart chakra, governing love, compassion, and emotional well-being. Its energy helps heal emotional wounds, encourage emotional balance, and foster a deeper connection with oneself and others. Malachite can assist in releasing negative emotions, promoting forgiveness, and nurturing self-love. It enhances manifestation abilities, helping to bring desires and goals into reality. Malachite can assist in clarifying intentions, aligning with one's true purpose, and manifesting positive outcomes.

Moldavite: This stone accelerates personal and spiritual growth, facilitating profound changes and shifts in consciousness. Moldavite can assist in breaking through limitations, opening doors to higher dimensions, and catalyzing spiritual awakening experiences. It can help dissolve energy blockages and release old patterns. Moldavite releases deep-seated emotional wounds, facilitates emotional healing, and supports the integration of shadow aspects. Moldavite can assist in healing on all levels—physical, emotional, mental, and spiritual.

Oils and Herbs

As with gemstones, oils and herbs can be used in many ways during the healing process. I like to use these specifically during difficult times while working through each energy field. Not only can you experience moments of intense emotion, you may also experience what's called a healing crisis. Sometimes during a healing crisis it can feel like you have flu-like symptoms. This is actually the toxins leaving the body. You can experience this after a reiki session or sometimes after a yoga sequence. There are other times you may experience a healing crisis, and in these instances, I find it useful to use the oils and herbs. This is also a good time to drink the tea blends.

Jasmine: This plant evokes feelings of passion, romance, and emotional intimacy. Jasmine can assist in opening the heart chakra, enhancing feelings of love and affection, and deepening connections in relationships. It represents feminine power, grace, and beauty. Jasmine can help in invoking and aligning with the qualities of the divine feminine, such as intuition, nurturing, and creativity. Jasmine is known for its calming and soothing effects on the mind and body. Its aroma is often used in aromatherapy to promote relaxation, reduce stress, and induce a state of tranquility. Jasmine can assist in calming the mind, relieving anxiety, and cultivating inner peace.

Rose: This is the flower of love, representing both romantic love and unconditional love. It is associated with the heart chakra and promotes feelings of love, compassion, and emotional healing. Rose assists in opening the heart, fostering deeper connections in relationships, and cultivating self-love. Rose represents grace, beauty, and nurturing qualities. Rose is associated with goddesses such as Venus, Aphrodite, and Mary, embodying feminine power and wisdom. It can assist in connecting with and embracing the divine feminine within oneself. Rose is associated with the concept of spiritual love and devotion to a higher power. Rose can assist in deepening spiritual practices, meditation, and prayer, fostering a sense of connection with the Divine. Rose is a symbol of spiritual growth, enlightenment, and the unfolding of consciousness. It is often associated with the lotus flower, representing spiritual awakening and the journey toward self-realization.

Yarrow: This herb enhances intuition, psychic abilities, and spiritual perception. Yarrow is associated with purification, detoxification, and the release of energetic blockages. Yarrow can assist in emotional healing, facilitating the processing and release of past traumas or emotional wounds.

Eucalyptus: This has an invigorating scent and is often used to clear stagnant or negative energies from a space, creating a fresh and revitalized environment. Eucalyptus can assist in purifying the aura, removing energetic blockages, and promoting a sense of clarity and renewal. It is known for its healing properties, particularly in relation to the respiratory system. Eucalyptus can be used to support emotional and energetic healing. Eucalyptus is used to energetically refresh and revitalize the body, mind, and spirit.

Shadow Work

The following practice is the flow I like to use when doing my own shadow work. There is no wrong way. Find what works for you and move at your own pace.

1. Where are your physical issues? If you have stomach issues, maybe start with the solar plexus. If you are not sure about what is physically out of alignment, I would simply start with the root and move up from there.

2. Once you decide which chakra you are going to start focusing on, put your energy and thoughts toward that chakra at night. Even before knowing what may come up, simply put your hands on that energy center as you fall asleep. You can send healing light visually to that chakra and say out loud or to yourself "I am ready to release any stuck and unhealed energy. I am ready to see what has been hiding in the shadows." Then be open to what happens next. Your days to follow will bring up issues you have been avoiding.

3. Set time aside weekly for processing the emotions, emotional reactions, triggers, and social interactions that are coming up. You may even want to do this daily before you go to bed. Start journaling the questions you are asking and answering for yourself.

4. Finally, decide which of the provided tools you will use and create a routine for each. Slowly integrate changes into your routine. Do not try to do everything all at once. In order to create sustainable lifestyle changes, you should start with one at a time. After you feel comfortable with steps two and three, maybe add drinking herbal teas or yoga once a week.

Questions for Heart Chakra Shadow Work

Grief is loss. We grieve because something that once held space in our hearts has gone and we feel the loss or the void. It can be a job, a relationship, even an expectation or a belief. However, when we recognize the love we feel for that job, relationship, or idea is really generated from ourselves and not from outside of us, we don't experience the loss. This is not about death; however, it can have a profound impact on the grief you feel when someone passes if you can realize the love and the connection is not lost. That takes a lot of work and practice to feel. These are hard truths you will have to face.

This is probably the chakra and the shadow work that took the longest for me to work through. I was very codependent with covert abandonment issues. My family lived with me, and my parents never divorced, but I was always alone. My sisters were teenagers when I was seven, my mom was chronically ill, and my father commuted to another state most of my childhood. That is why I say *covert* abandonment issues. It was very hard to identify why I always felt so alone. Once I dug down deep enough by read-ing and being part of healing communities, I found the core of the loneliness in my heart and was able to start rebuilding the void.

I honestly never knew I could feel so complete within myself. For forty-two years, no matter who came into or out of my life, I had a loneliness that no one could fill, even my children. No matter how hard I tried to attach myself to love and relationships, noth-ing felt complete. Not until I started to do the shadow work, and especially not until I got to my heart, could I feel what I feel now. I started by saying affirmations, simple things like "I am loved." That alone didn't get me to where I am now, but what it did do was help me start hearing the love. For the first time, I could hear people who expressed love for me. I could hear gratitude. I started to accept the compliments. I started to believe people when they told me I helped them or that they wanted to be around me. This was something I struggled believing my entire life. Now I say, "I love," and I have become what I want to receive, and I receive with ease because of that.

During my healing process I still chose a toxic partner, but he mirrored me. I had started to see myself, and when it was over, I had become complete because I never gave up on myself. Nothing was lost, only different.

While studying the yoga sutras, one really hit hard for me and changed my world:

> In the absence of the state of mind called Yoga, the ability to understand the object is simply replaced by the mind's conception of that object or by a total lack of comprehension. A disturbed mind can rarely follow a direction. If it ever does, comprehension of the object will be faulty.[3]

To me, this is stating that we cannot clearly see our reality when we are "disturbed," reacting from a place of fear and survival. We cannot comprehend when our mind is fragmented or living in the past. This also speaks to how we cannot see our true self, which led me to connect with Sutra 1.4 below.

> At all other times, the Self appears to assume the form of thought's vacillations and the True Self is lost.[4]

---

3. T. K. V. Desikachar, *The Heart of Yoga: Developing a Personal Practice* (Rochester, VT: Inner Traditions, 1995), 150.

4. Mukunda Stiles, interpreter, *Yoga Sutras of Patanjali* (Boston, MA: RedWheel/Weister, 2002), 2.

My interpretation after attending and participating in much class discussion is this: when lost in the stories, the true self is also lost. The illusion becomes reality. I was lost in the story of being unlovable. I was lost in the story that people saw me as different, a freak, or even evil. I had a constant running dialogue in the back of my mind that had slipped from my conscious mind into my unconscious mind. It vibrated out of me and became the illusion of my reality. It became the story I was attracted to over and over again even though I no longer could hear the script. I never let it go, so it lived in my shadows. It is not easy to look at what lies in the shadows of our heart, but it is worth it when you realize you are the unconditional love that you feel.

Letter for Heart Chakra Shadow Work

Doing heart-centered work has no best time. You can and should work on loving yourself unconditionally. Every night before bed, during your morning routine—there is no time that is not good. This is the most powerful energy source when dealing with your overall joy and perception of the life you are living. Place your hands in the center of your chest and read your letter to yourself as often as you can. Watch how your life changes! Here's an example:

Every day in every way, I am loved. I feel love always in all ways. Today and every day, I create a life full of unconditional love that releases and heals all stories and attachments that have caused suffering in my heart. I do all things with love. I feel the feast of life and living, and I embrace the cornucopia on my plate.

Letters to Write to Yourself When Healing the Heart

What are my attachments? What behaviors and actions have caused me to hold onto things, perceptions, expectations, stories, or people that I should have let go of long ago? Where is the void in my heart? Am I ready and willing to fill the void with my own unconditional love and release all attachments?

When I write letters to my heart, I address them to God. In the past when I hadn't healed my relationship with that word or that energy, I would use the name Rachel. The word *God* has created a lot of trauma on this planet, and if it makes you uncomfortable, please use a name or an energy that works for you. I was able to heal the use of that word during my yoga studies. It became an energy instead of a person judging me. However, when people ask me what I believe in, I will still say love. Love is the energy that governs our hearts, and love is what we are speaking to. It is our heart that connects and fills the voids. I have found that when I know I am connected to a higher energy and I know all things are connected to me, it allows me to heal faster. It's a matter of remembering.

Dear God, I have held onto painful memories and painful versions of myself for too long. I am releasing them to the universe to take and transmute back into love. I know that I am nothing but energy in motion and each moment is as important as the next. I will be present of mind and heart, and I choose life with an open mind and an open heart. I will let go of any moment, person, place, or image that is ending.

I have held space for everyone else's heart and needs. I have given my time and attention to the wrong people too many times. I am focused on filling my own heart and becoming an example of how to fully recover from darkness. I will allow myself to shine and be seen at all times. I am rewriting my life every moment.

Affirmations for Heart Chakra Energy Work

I love! I love unconditionally!

I love each moment with an open heart and an open mind!

Recipes for Heart Chakra Energy Work

For each tea blend, I use loose-leaf herbs and tea leaves and make the blends in 20-ounce Mason jars. I use about ⅓ of a cup for each ingredient. I gently roll the Mason jar to mix the ingredients together without breaking up the herbs into dust.

When I'm ready to brew the tea, I heat up water in a teapot and scoop a tablespoon of the blend into a reusable tea bag. I then add my tea bag plus other ingredients such as honey or lemon (to taste) to a mug before the water is done. When the water is hot, I add it to the mug slowly.

To activate the tea with the incantation, I do a few things: First, I will write the incantation onto a sticky note and put it on the pot as it heats the water. As I pour the water slowly, I will read the incantation out loud. I stop the pour with enough room at the top of my mug so that the next part does not cause the water to spill out. Once the water is a little cooled down, I will place my right hand over the top of the mug and grasp it (not by its handle but by the rim) so that the energy from my hand is also infused into the water. Once I have a firm grip, I will pick it up and swirl the mug and tea clockwise three times while saying the incantation. I will also repeat this on my left side three times but counterclockwise. Then I will go back to my right hand and repeat the swirl but counterclockwise then left hand clockwise.

Your tea is now fully infused with the energy you intend, and once it is cooled down enough to drink, enjoy.

Love Potion Tea and Incantation

- Chocolate Pu'er, damiana, dried strawberries, rosebuds, mint

"Water of desire and passion, let romance grow. Open heart and open mind. The path of love will show from within and above. Waters flowing through me bring me love."

Connected Tea and Incantation

- Green tea, butterfly pea, jasmine, lemon peel, mint

"In my heart and in my soul, I am one with creation, connected to all. I am the holy spirit around me and within me, as above, so below."

Movement and Yoga Sequence for the Heart

Balancing and opening your heart chakra can be done every day, whether you put your hands on your heart, say a few affirmations, do a meditation, or these yoga poses; there is always something you can do to feel more love. An open heart allows us to see light in the dark and can prolong your life. During this or any yoga sequence, see light pouring into your heart as you hold each pose for five or more seconds. Believe me, it will change your life.

1. **Sun Salutation (Surya Namaskar):**
   - Start in mountain pose (tadasana) with your feet together and palms at your heart center.
   - Inhale, raise your arms overhead, and gently arch back (upward salute / urdhva hastasana).
   - Exhale, fold forward from your hips (forward fold / uttanasana), bending your knees if needed.

- Inhale, lengthen your spine, and lift your chest halfway (halfway lift / ardha uttanasana).
- Exhale, step or jump back into plank pose, aligning your wrists under your shoulders.
- Lower your body halfway down with bent elbows (chaturanga dandasana).
- Inhale, lift your chest, and gaze upward, coming into upward-facing dog (urdhva mukha svanasana).
- Exhale, lift your hips, and press back into downward-facing dog (adho mukha svanasana).
- Hold for a few breaths, then step or jump your feet between your hands.
- Inhale, lift your chest halfway (halfway lift / ardha uttanasana).
- Exhale, fold forward (forward fold / uttanasana).
- Inhale, sweep your arms out to the sides, and come up, reaching overhead (upward salute / urdhva hastasana).
- Exhale, bring your palms together at your heart center (mountain pose / tadasana).

2. **Standing Backbend (Ardha Chakrasana):**
   - Stand tall in mountain pose with your feet hip-width apart.
   - Place your hands on your lower back with your fingers pointing downward.
   - Inhale, lift your chest, and gently arch backward, extending your spine.
   - Keep your gaze upward or slightly behind you.

- Engage your core and keep your legs active.
- Hold the pose for a few breaths, feeling a gentle stretch in your front body.

3. **King Dancer Pose (Natarajasana):**
- Shift into mountain pose.
- From mountain pose, shift your weight onto your left foot.
- Bend your right knee and reach back with your right hand to grasp your right ankle or foot.
- Inhale, lift your left arm up and extend it forward.
- Kick your right foot into your hand and simultaneously extend your right leg straight back.
- Keep your chest lifted and gaze forward.
- Hold the pose for a few breaths, finding balance and focus.
- Release the pose and repeat on the other side.

4. **Sun Salutation (Surya Namaskar):**
- Repeat the Sun Salutation sequence described in step 1.

5. **Cat-Cow Pose (Marjaryasana-Bitilasana):**
- Come onto all fours with your hands under your shoulders and knees under your hips.
- Inhale, arch your back, and lift your tailbone, bringing your gaze upward (cow pose / bitilasana).
- Exhale, round your spine, tuck your chin toward your chest, and engage your core (cat pose / marjaryasana).
- Flow between these two poses with your breath, moving with a gentle and fluid motion.

- Continue for several rounds, focusing on the movement of your spine.

6. **Camel Pose (Ustrasana):**
   - Kneel on the mat with your knees hip-width apart.
   - Place your hands on your lower back, fingers pointing downward.
   - Inhale, lift your chest, and gently arch backward, reaching your hands toward your heels.
   - Keep your neck relaxed and gaze upward or slightly behind you.
   - Engage your core and thighs, and press your hips forward.
   - Hold the pose for a few breaths, feeling a deep opening in your chest and hips.

7. **Sun Salutation (Surya Namaskar):**
   - Repeat the Sun Salutation sequence described in step 1.

8. **Child's Pose (Balasana):**
   - Kneel on the floor, bringing your big toes together and sitting back on your heels.
   - Exhale, fold your torso forward, and rest your forehead on the mat.
   - Extend your arms forward or rest them by your sides.
   - Allow your body to relax completely, surrendering to the pose.
   - Stay in this pose for a few breaths, focusing on deep relaxation.

9. **Corpse Pose (Savasana):**
   - Lie flat on your back with your legs extended and arms by your sides.
   - Close your eyes and let go of any tension in your body.
   - Relax your entire body and surrender to the pose.
   - Stay in this pose for several minutes, focusing on deep rest and rejuvenation.

Remember to listen to your body and modify the poses as needed. If you're new to yoga or have any specific concerns, it's a good idea to seek guidance from a qualified yoga instructor. Enjoy your practice!

Meditations

Start with the centering and grounding meditation you've been practicing since the root chakra, open up the soul star above your head, and start the visualization of energy moving through the chakras as you've done before. Remember to bring the celestial healing light and the healing earth energy up and around your extended aura. This time you are not going to travel to a guided space. You are just going to sit in the energy and prepare to do a mala meditation.

Mala Meditation

Mala beads are a string of 108 beads, plus 1 guru bead, a tassel or charm, and sometimes a few larger beads to indicate a pause or a breath. One hundred and eight is considered a sacred number in many different cultures. These 108 beads are your markers for the intention you will focus on silently or out loud like a chant. These beads are commonly made of gemstones, which will enhance the vibration of the intention and mantra you are setting. Traditionally, malas have been made of the Rudraksha seed, which is believed to protect people from negativity while seeking a higher spiritual plane. Mala prayer is commonly used in Buddhist cultures and by yogis; however, many people have come to see the power and embraced the belief and tradition of meditation with mala beads.

To get started, you will want to find a mala necklace that speaks to you through color, stone, or traditional wood. You may already have an intention or mantra in mind. The first set of mala beads I was drawn to were amazonite beads. I did not have an intention or mantra in mind at the time, but I was drawn to the beautiful ocean blue color of the stones. As I read about what energies amazonite promotes, I found that I wanted to use the words "I am connected"—simple words. The repetition of the mantra 108 times not only has a spiritual effect on your energy, but it also has a scientific effect on the body, mind, and spirit. Saying something in repetition creates a belief system in the body. Many institutions use repetition to create a solid, unbreakable belief system. You want to pick a mantra that aligns to your true being. "I am connected" is simple yet has the intention of creating a connection to source or God energy. I do not have to specify that part because I know what I mean when I say it. However, you should be as specific as possible.

Once you start to believe the mantra you are saying, you have opened your reticular activating system (RAS) in the mind. The RAS is a network of interconnected nuclei and neural pathways located in the brainstem. It plays a crucial role in regulating arousal and sleep-wake transitions. The RAS acts as a filter for incoming sensory information, determining which stimuli to pay attention to and which to ignore.

This is the area of our brain where we pick up the images around us. When you don't see something in your environment that someone else clearly saw, it's because your RAS was closed off to it. Subconsciously you didn't believe, and therefore your brain never registered the situation. Once your RAS is open to the energy or reality you are trying to bring into your life, you will start to see it show up. You will now be able to see possibilities and open doors that you were once blind to. Then your mirror neurons kick in and show you this new vision of your reality. Your mirror neurons will see the people who are emanating the energy you wish to create, and they will mimic the vibration from your own body. You will begin to project what you want. This is why mantras and affirmations are so powerful.

First you say it. Then you believe it. Then you see it. Then you become it.

Pick your mala beads, pick your mantra, and begin at the guru bead. Once you have done your centering and grounding visualization, the same as you've been doing since the root chakra, you are set to start the meditation. You will hold the mala with one hand starting at the guru bead, and you will recite silently or out loud your mantra on each bead as they run through your fingers. When you reach a pause, reflect and breathe on the energy you are creating. Refocus here if your mind has wandered. Once you reach the guru bead again, you may choose to end your mantra meditation, or you may choose to continue. However, if you choose to continue, turn the beads around and go back the way you came. You don't want to pass over the guru bead and close the circle. You want the energy to be open so it can go where it needs to.

The Heart Activation

You are going to listen to your heart and ask questions about what it is the heart really wants. You may not be able to know with certainty what exactly it is the heart wants at first. When it comes to specifics, the heart tends to change its mind too often, which is why I suggest listening for the simplest answer when asking the heart what it wants. While doing this most recently, I simply asked, "What do you need to feel full again?" My heart responded, "I want more freedom." So that is what I focused on.

Put your hands on your heart and visualize light pouring from the palms of your hands straight into your heart. You do not need to be a healer of any kind to activate the healing energy in your hands when it comes to healing yourself. As you feel this energy open your heart, say, "I am free" or whatever your words will be. You could also use "I am love." That will activate your heart no matter what your desire is. Even more powerful are the words "I am the great I am." These words connect you to universal source energy or God. Visualize those words and that light pushing out into your aura, creating the flow of love energy through each layer of your aura—physical, emotional, spiritual, wisdom, and bliss energy bodies. Once you reach the bliss layer of your auric field, you may choose to see a diamond on the outermost layer of energy. This is a protective layer so that you may expand as far as you want.

Doing this every day, morning and night, will help you feel whole and complete. You will start to see that you are relying less and less on outer circumstances to fill a void. You will notice there no longer is a void. You will notice that you *are* unconditional love. You are the feeling you have searched for all along. You will begin to believe you no longer need any attachments. You will begin to be fully present at any moment. You will allow the grieving process of anything that has ended to move through you gracefully.

What your life will become once you feel whole within your own heart will amaze you. This is the space we occupy when we think of the saying "don't sweat the small stuff" or when we think about living our lives in compliance with *The Four Agreements* by don Miguel Ruiz, or at least the agreement that states "don't take anything personally."[5] You begin to really live knowing everyone is only ever thinking about themselves no matter how much of a healer or servant to this earth they are. The background script always puts us first. This is not selfish; this is human nature, and once we learn to take care of ourselves first, we can be fully present for others. This becomes the great I am!

Rituals

The rituals for the heart chakra are all about unconditional love toward yourself and others. We are working from the heart center and radiating the energy throughout the whole body.

Love Light

The most common spellwork you see from the heart center is hands in prayer position at the center of the chest. This prayer position is actually a mudra. A *mudra* is a symbolic gesture made with the hands and is typically found in yoga, Buddhism, and Hinduism. However, prayer position used in Christian faiths is also a mudra and so are the hand gestures made by Baphomet to sign the divine feminine and divine masculine.

---

5. Don Miguel Ruiz, *The Four Agreements*, with Janet Mills (San Rafael, CA: Amber-Allen Publishing, 1997), 47.

The arms and the hands are extensions of the heart energy, and any mudra you use to activate the intended energy will be coming from the heart center. The most well-known mudras are used during meditation practices as a way to channel the flow of life force energy or source energy. Mudras are a nonverbal form of communication and self-expression. They are used to activate the mind to connect to divine powers or the deities themselves just as prayer hands activate the connection that you are communicating with the God energy.

There are many different mudras you can find; however, the three I like to use most often are prayer position, anahata, and the signs of Baphomet. Prayer position, putting your hands together with palms touching and then placing them on your heart, activates a portal to universal love and sends energy to you. Anahata is when the right hand and left both have the index finger and the thumb touching. The right hand is at the heart center, and the left hand sits on the knee. This mudra symbolizes a connection to the physical and energetic heart. Both of these are good when dealing with matters of the heart. Sit in a meditation position and allow yourself to mindfully have a conversation with your heart while your hands are in these mudras, and you will activate what it is you desire.

Restoring the Heart

Working with a more specific intention to restore balance in my heart, I will use the hand gestures made by the Baphomet. Both hands hold the index and middle finger up while the thumb covers the pinky and the ring finger. The right hand is held bent at the elbow upward and the left hand is held downward. The left hand receives energy and is the divine feminine side while the right hand gives energy and is the divine masculine. These mudras also represent "as above so below," activating the two polarities of heaven and earth, the balance of mercy and justice, the waxing and waning of the moon. The mudra of the Baphomet activates the balance of life. I use this in my meditations when I desire balance to be restored.

Your Turn

There are many different mudras, and they can be used to enhance any intention. Mudras can be very powerful ways to create an energetic portal. You can create any ritual you want by choosing a mudra, sitting with your legs crossed, and focusing on the energy and the intention you want.

Psychic Center of the Heart

This is a common psychic energy most of us feel. This is where we get empaths from. The heart feels others' emotions so intensely that sometimes they can be interpreted as your own. Empaths have to really be cognizant of what is theirs and what is other people's. It can be very overwhelming for an empath to be in crowded spaces because their heart center is overwhelmed with each and every person's emotional disposition. Empaths have to work really hard at learning to keep others' emotions out yet still be able to read and respond to them.

The empath can feel depressed if in a relationship with someone who is depressed. They tend to absorb the energies of those they love, interpreting them as their own. They can even be misdiagnosed if they are in a close relationship with someone who has an emotional diagnosis. It is very important for an empath to learn about their own energy and to set boundaries.

As an empath, it can be effective to visualize a diamond around your auric layers. I explain this grid as a honeycomb or the force field you see in Marvel movies. It is a series of hexagons connected together and layered. I have found this to be the most effective form of protection, and I visualize it every day around anything I want protected.

However, your boundaries also have to be expressed clearly. Empaths can pick up on the most hidden of emotions, but not everyone out there is hiding their emotions. Some of them use emotions to manipulate energy, and an empath can easily get caught in this sort of web, which is why we often see empaths with narcissists. A narcissist will mirror back to the empath the purest parts of the heart coming from the empath. An empath who hasn't learned about themselves will confuse the light they see from the narcissist as the narcissist, when in reality, it is their own light. The empath is essentially falling in love with themselves. Once this is realized, life becomes a lot brighter for the empath.

However, being an empath also comes with superpowers. Empaths make people feel heard and validated. An empath can make people feel like they are not alone, sometimes for the first time in their lives. This can be very healing for many people. People are drawn to empaths and will tell them everything because they can feel and connect to an empath's heart. They won't know this is what is actually happening, but it is. The heart space of an empath is wide open, like arms hugging others' hearts. Because of this, empaths are natural healers. The open heart space allows the empath to create a connection, oftentimes through some form of art or teaching that others feel moved by. Think of a musician who "just speaks to you."

Lastly, an empath is also a human lie detector. They know when the information is not matching the vibration. They also know when there is more to the story than what is being told. They can feel the lack of information. Because this is such a heightened quality for empaths, many people will try to suggest that the empath is crazy in order to throw them off the trail. However, the more an empath trusts themselves, the harder it becomes for people to manipulate an empath. Having an open heart space is a very powerful thing and should be cultivated with clear awareness.

Chapter Six
Throat Chakra, Vishuddha

Located right at the center of the throat is the energy for communication, and this balances your ability to communicate effectively and with authenticity. It's not just about saying words but the honesty that you speak. The throat can become blocked if you are not saying what you need to say or if you are saying things that are out of balance with your truth. This energy center is commonly blocked. It seems to be one that we most often treat harshly. We feel seen when we speak, and if we are not ready to be seen, we hold back our voice. Either we don't speak up for ourselves or we say what we think people want to hear. It takes a lot of work on the lower chakras to put this one back into balance. We have to work on our self-awareness and acceptance before we can truly speak our honesty and allow ourselves to show vulnerability. We have to know that our foundation (root chakra) and our core (sacral chakra) won't be disrupted when we share our truth. We also must have the courage (solar plexus chakra) and love ourselves (heart chakra) enough to know showing up with our truth is an essential part of healing.

We tend to abuse our throat chakra the most, maybe because we think it hides our most vulnerable parts. The throat is our representative. It is where we have elected in the energy system to make sure we are being treated fairly, to make sure we are being taken care of, but oftentimes we do not let our representative do its job. We don't know how we want to show up or what parts of ourselves we want to speak on behalf of, so we stay quiet or just regurgitate what we've heard from others rather than risk exposure of our true self. If we are not ready to be seen, we will lie to cover up our most vulnerable parts, which will only create more shame.

We want to learn to get to a place where we can express our truth with ease. It is important to note it is *our* truth, not *the* truth. We are allowing your personal truth to flow here. The throat chakra is not simply about speaking but about communication as an entire flow of energy, which includes actively listening. This is when we listen to the words, the emotions, the energy not being expressed, and we respond. We don't jump to what we think is being said. We learn to speak and listen mindfully when our throat chakra is healed and balanced.

I Speak

"I speak" emphasizes the capacity to express thoughts, feelings, and ideas clearly and honestly. Most of us have the ability to talk and communicate, but are we truly doing our best at this? Do we listen not only to what is being said to us by others but also to what we are saying to ourselves? This is when it becomes important to decipher our different voices. Through my work, it has become clear we all have a voice of truth, a voice of fight or flight, and a voice of inquiry. We need to be able to feel the difference between these voices within our body. I have discovered in my own body that the voice of truth enters from the right and slightly higher than the voice of fight or flight, which comes in on the left. The voice of inquiry is directly at the center of my mind. I have recognized these also correspond with the voices of spirit, ego, and telepathy. Once you discover how your body receives these voices, you will have a much easier time communicating your truth.

Tools and Properties of the Throat for Alignment

Emotional connections: Communication, expression (artistic and personal), voice, honesty, authenticity, purpose, independence

Physical connections: Neck, top of spine, throat, vocal cords, mouth, teeth, tongue, thyroid, speech, endocrine system, shoulders, upper arms, trapezius muscles

Foods: Blueberries, blackberries, coconut water, raw honey, herbal teas, figs, kelp, blue algae, blue corn, black cherries, eggplant, purple cabbage

Activities: Singing, screaming, humming

Color: Blue—The throat responds to blues and balances when fed blue foods.

Element: Space—Humming while looking up at the stars can bring balance to the throat chakra.

Tones and notes: G, eeh—Listening to music, sounds, and frequencies that have these in them can break up blocks and clear out energy. Attend a sound healing class or listen to frequencies on any music app.

Gemstones

Gemstones have many uses for healing and vibrational alignment. They are widely used in holistic practices among many cultures. If you choose to work on one chakra at a time the way this book is laid out, you may want to wear gemstones as jewelry to create a vibrational frequency that aligns to the energy you are moving through. However, you can use them during meditation either on an altar or placed upon the chakra you are working with. You may want to set a routine for this type of meditation or for when you are in the middle of experiencing the emotions. Setting multiple gemstones together around the house in a patterned grid amplifies the energy you are working with and creates movement of this energy. You can do this during the entire cycle of working with this chakra, then change the grid when you move to the next chakra.

Lapis lazuli: This stone enhances effective communication, both verbal and written, and promotes confident self-expression. Lapis lazuli assists in speaking one's truth, expressing emotions, and facilitating clear and authentic communication with others. It harmonizes the body, mind, and spirit, promoting overall well-being. Lapis lazuli is often associated with seeking truth, wisdom, and spiritual knowledge. It is believed to stimulate intellectual curiosity and inspire deep reflection. Lapis lazuli assists in uncovering hidden knowledge, gaining insights into the self and the universe, and fostering spiritual growth and expansion.

Aquamarine: This stone promotes a sense of tranquility, relaxation, and inner peace. Aquamarine is associated with enhancing communication and self-expression. It opens up the throat chakra. Aquamarine assists in expressing oneself with confidence, articulating thoughts and emotions, and promoting harmonious communication with others. Aquamarine brings a sense of peace, harmony, and balance to relationships, environments, and inner experiences.

Chrysocolla: This stone facilitates clear and heartfelt communication, both in verbal and written forms. Chrysocolla can assist in expressing one's thoughts, emotions, and needs with compassion, confidence, and authenticity. It encourages self-reflection, introspection, and the exploration of one's inner truth. Chrysocolla can assist in gaining insight into one's own needs, desires, and life purpose, fostering personal growth and self-discovery. Chrysocolla facilitates physical healing, particularly in the areas of the throat, heart, and emotional body. Chrysocolla can assist in releasing energetic blockages and promoting self-healing.

Turquoise: This stone enhances effective and honest communication, both in verbal and nonverbal forms. Turquoise can assist in expressing oneself with clarity, assertiveness, and compassion. It is also associated with fostering creativity and artistic expression. Turquoise is known to support spiritual growth and awareness. It opens the channels of intuition, enhances psychic abilities, and promotes a deeper connection with higher realms. Turquoise can assist in expanding consciousness, accessing spiritual insights, and aligning with one's spiritual path. Turquoise enhances communication between the physical and spiritual and stabilizes the thyroid.

Larimar: Often referred to as the "stone of serenity" due to its calming and soothing energy, it promotes a sense of tranquility, relaxation, and inner peace. Larimar can assist in reducing stress, anxiety, and emotional turmoil, allowing for a greater sense of balance and well-being. Larimar is the wisdom of the sea, quiet confidence, and clear communication. Larimar is associated with enhancing communication and self-expression. Larimar can assist in expressing one's thoughts, emotions, and needs with clarity, confidence, and compassion. It can also aid in speaking one's truth and promoting harmonious communication with others. Larimar promotes empathy, understanding, and compassion toward oneself and others. Larimar can assist in developing a deeper connection with one's own emotions and the emotions of others.

Angelite: This stone facilitates communication with angelic beings and spirit guides. It is said to help establish a stronger connection to the angelic realm, enabling individuals to receive guidance, support, and messages from higher realms. Angelite helps individuals tune in to their inner wisdom, expand their consciousness, and access higher realms of knowledge and understanding. Angelite is said to facilitate clear self-expression. It can assist in effective and authentic communication, helping individuals express their thoughts, feelings, and needs with clarity and compassion. Angelite may also aid in harmonious communication within relationships and promote assertiveness.

Sodalite: This stone enhances effective communication, both in verbal and written forms. Sodalite can assist in expressing oneself with clarity, confidence, and authenticity, fostering harmonious and honest communication. Sodalite is said to encourage self-exploration and self-acceptance. It assists individuals in uncovering and embracing their true selves, promoting self-awareness and personal growth. Sodalite may support individuals in recognizing and releasing self-limiting beliefs or patterns.

Blue lace agate: Associated with enhancing communication and self-expression, this stone helps individuals express their thoughts and feelings with clarity and ease, promoting effective and honest communication. Blue lace agate is particularly beneficial for those who struggle with communication blocks or fear of speaking their truth. It has a gentle and nurturing energy that aids in emotional healing. It assists in releasing emotional wounds, soothing emotional pain, and promoting emotional stability. Blue lace agate is often used to alleviate feelings of anger, resentment, and bitterness, encouraging forgiveness and compassion. Blue lace agate is believed to bring balance and harmony to one's inner being. It can help align the mind, body, and spirit, promoting a sense of overall well-being. Blue lace agate is associated with harmonizing energy flow, enhancing self-awareness, and fostering inner harmony.

Blue kyanite: This stone aligns and balances the chakras, particularly the throat and third eye chakras. It can help restore energetic balance and clear any blockages in these energy centers, allowing for improved communication, self-expression, and intuitive abilities. Blue kyanite assists individuals in speaking their truth with clarity, confidence, and authenticity. Blue kyanite may also help improve listening skills and promote effective communication in relationships. It encourages introspection, self-awareness, and personal growth. Blue kyanite may assist individuals in gaining clarity about their life path, purpose, and inner desires.

Oils and Herbs

As with gemstones, oils and herbs can be used in many ways during the healing process. I like to use these specifically during difficult times while working through each energy field. Not only can you experience moments of intense emotion, you may also experience what's called a healing crisis. Sometimes during a healing crisis it can feel like you have flu-like symptoms. This is actually the toxins leaving the body. You can experience this after a reiki session or sometimes after a yoga sequence. There are other times you may experience a healing crisis, and in these instances, I find it useful to use the oils and herbs. This is also a good time to drink the tea blends.

Chamomile: Well known to calm the mind, ease stress and anxiety, and promote a state of inner tranquility, chamomile assists individuals in accessing their intuition, trusting their instincts, and making decisions from a place of inner knowing. Chamomile is often used to facilitate spiritual insight and clarity. It alleviates feelings of irritability, tension, or sadness, promoting emotional balance and well-being. Chamomile is often used as part of self-care rituals to nurture and support emotional healing.

Sage: This herb clears negative or stagnant energies from a space, object, or person. Sage is often used in smoke rituals, where the smoke is used to purify the energy and create a sacred atmosphere. Sage helps individuals gain insights, connect with higher guidance, and access deeper levels of understanding. Sage is often used in meditation or spiritual practices to facilitate spiritual growth and awareness. Be mindful that sage is overharvested. Try to buy from Indigenous communities.

Clove: This spice has strong protective properties. It is often used to ward off negative energies, evil spirits, and unwanted influences. Clove is considered a powerful tool for cleansing and purifying spaces, objects, and individuals. It stops negative communication and gossip and enhances spiritual vibrations.

Cedarwood: This oil facilitates a deeper connection with the Divine, higher realms, and spiritual guidance. Cedarwood enhances inner wisdom, intuition, and spiritual insight. Cedarwood is often used to foster personal growth, boost confidence, and support decision-making from a place of inner knowing. Cedarwood is used to bless and consecrate sacred spaces, altars, or spiritual tools. It is believed to infuse the environment with positive energy and create a sacred atmosphere.

Yarrow: This herb promotes clear communication and enhances the ability to express oneself authentically. It can assist in removing energetic blocks in the throat chakra, improving communication skills, and promoting honest self-expression.

Shadow Work

The following practice is the flow I like to use when doing my own shadow work. There is no wrong way. Find what works for you and move at your own pace.

1. Where are your physical issues? If you have stomach issues, maybe start with the solar plexus. If you are not sure about what is physically out of alignment, I would simply start with the root and move up from there.

2. Once you decide which chakra you are going to start focusing on, put your energy and thoughts toward that chakra at night. Even before knowing what may come up, simply put your hands on that energy center as you

fall asleep. You can send healing light visually to that chakra and say out loud or to yourself "I am ready to release any stuck and unhealed energy. I am ready to see what has been hiding in the shadows." Then be open to what happens next. Your days to follow will bring up issues you have been avoiding.

3. Set time aside weekly for processing the emotions, emotional reactions, triggers, and social interactions that are coming up. You may even want to do this daily before you go to bed. Start journaling the questions you are asking and answering for yourself.

4. Finally, decide which of the provided tools you will use and create a routine for each. Slowly integrate changes into your routine. Do not try to do everything all at once. In order to create sustainable lifestyle changes, you should start with one at a time. After you feel comfortable with steps two and three, maybe add drinking herbal teas or yoga once a week.

Questions for Throat Chakra Shadow Work

Being able to find your truth, let alone speak it, comes with a lot of unraveling of your beliefs. It takes strength and courage and a willingness to open your heart to unconditional love. We may even know our truth. It might already be screaming and gnawing at us, but living it and speaking it are something much, much more powerful. I get excited at the potential for an aligned energy source and how it will transform your life, but being able to fully allow your throat chakra to be in its power and alignment is more life changing than you can imagine. Everything becomes real! Everything you worked to heal and align and achieve becomes real once you are working with your throat's power center.

The throat chakra is not just about speaking or finding your voice. The throat chakra is your truth—listen for it, open up to it, let it bleed from you. Many of us are trying to avoid short-term conflict by choosing to speak half-truths or non-truths to "keep the peace." This never keeps the peace; it only prolongs the conflict or the discomfort, and it disturbs your actual peace for a very long time. When you engage in these types of short-term lies or lies of omission, the truth will still come out. You will grow resentful of yourself or the person you perceive has created this cycle. However, it is always you that has created the cycle. If you can speak your truth fully and in the first moment it arises, you only bring more truth into your life. Without that, you become untrustworthy to yourself and everyone around you.

I had expressed to my family during a breakup that I was scared. They asked me what I was scared of. In the past I would have said I don't know, but this time I knew what I was afraid of. The awareness and the ability to speak of my fear took its power away. The very act of saying it out loud took the fear away.

Throat chakra energy is our source of honesty; it's the power of removing anything and everything that drains our energy and prevents us from being in a state of energy exchange and flow. The throat chakra is not where we are getting divine downloads or channeling from a place outside of ourselves. The truth we seek here is embedded in our body. It has become part of our DNA. This is where we can begin to unlock the scripts running in the background. The throat chakra is probably the most personal to who we are. Being able to speak our truth is essential in order to change our future and become a new, healed version of ourselves.

Ask yourself, what have I justified in my life that I truly don't believe? Really listen to your truth when you make a decision. Do you say yes when you mean no? You tell yourself you really want to go to that show when you don't. You might not even like the event in question, but you like the people. The less you speak your truth, the less you show up for yourself, and the less you show up for yourself, the more you attract what is wrong for you. Slow down and listen to every moment. Where is your truth?

What are you really feeling? This is the key to discovering the feelings running in the background, controlling the show, controlling the manifestations. It's not enough to say, "Every day in every way I am getting richer" if there is a voice saying, "No you aren't; you aren't worthy. You will suffer forever." Find that voice! Do not ignore it! Bring it from the shadows and listen! If you do not address the truth hidden deep in your emotional body, you will not be able to change your reality.

Most people will look at this as focusing on the negative, and that is not true at all. Ignoring the truth will never set you free. Fierce honesty about how you feel and how you are going to change those limiting beliefs becomes the positive. Men taught me I wasn't capable of taking care of myself. I have proven to myself time and time again that I can take care of myself, but my emotional truth is still that I can't take care of myself. I keep going back to places that are unsafe because of that emotional belief system—that thing I believe to be true.

So how will I change this truth? I need to ask myself, How did I see myself before they made me small? What lies in the shadows behind the shadows? Where is *my* truth behind everyone else's nurtured realities? Where is my voice? We have to look for the clues we've been trying to give ourselves our entire lives. As you were drowning your voice, you were simultaneously leaving yourself breadcrumbs. For me, it was a big tattoo across my back. I put the word *freedom* on my back twenty-two years ago and have been searching for that truth ever since. Freedom has always been my truth. Now it is time to fiercely live and speak my truth.

During the time I was working on this section of the book (the throat chakra), a man had entered my life. For a month we grew to know each other, spending long hours on the phone and, dare I say it, even falling in love. The problem was I had just left a long-term relationship, and I knew with all my heart I was not ready for what was happening. I had not completed, maybe even started, the grieving process from the relationship that had just ended. The connection was intense and perfect on so many levels, but there was a voice—a voice that I could hear being gentle and kind. A voice that was saying to me, "It's not time."

I knew this voice was not fear. As a matter of fact, the part I feared the most was not listening to the voice. I have an incredible ability to shove that voice down and cover it with beautifully crafted excuses. I also knew this voice was not trauma. I knew it wasn't trauma because trauma screams at you. It puts your body into fight or flight and activates survival mode. I was not in any of that.

I was simply hearing my truth, a truth I desperately wanted to ignore. The truth will get louder if you force it to. The truth will start to show up in your body if you force it to. However, the truth will always give you the chance to use it as power. It will always show up to guide you and show you the way. It's up to you to decide when you are going to listen, because it never goes away. You can listen when she first shows up, saving yourself and possibly others a lot of pain, or you can wait until she is tearing you apart.

During this time, I expressed to a friend that I had buyer's remorse over something I had bought. He didn't ask me, "Why do you regret it?" or support me and say, "It's fine; you'll love it."

He simply said, "What are you missing in your life that caused you to buy that?" I heard that question loud and clear. I heard it like it had dropped me on my ass from a thirty-foot cliff. I was grieving and I was using retail therapy to do it. I had not acknowledged this truth about myself before. I had used a bouquet of "reasons" why I needed things when I went through a big grieving process in my life.

Forty-seven years of life, I had no idea I had a retail therapy coping mechanism. This was a truth I discovered because I allowed myself to really be present with my mind and listen to the covered shadow that I had hidden away. Not only had I hidden it, I became an expert at disguises. I became a communications major in college and started teaching and coaching, becoming the woman who gets complimented for seeing the truth and communicating it so well. Ah ha! Fooled you! It was your truth I could see and communicate, not my own. I had made my weakness a false superpower. The truth is, this is my most toxic chakra, and no one would ever know it. It has been extremely hard to let the truth out. However, once I speak my truth and risk the pain of the moment, no matter how it plays out, I win the internal war. I hear my truth, and I don't need proof. I just need my voice.

Letter for Throat Chakra Shadow Work

Throat-centered work should be done as often as possible. Think about it like coming off autopilot. Stop allowing your conditioned responses to be what you speak. Pause to listen for your truth, then use your voice to speak it. You can and should work on the truth every single moment of every single day. This is the most powerful energy source when desiring to change your reality. The more you decode your truth, the closer you get to living it. Place your hands above your head, palms up and open. (This opens you up energetically.) And then read your letter out loud as often as you can. Watch how your life changes! Here's an example:

> *Every day, every way I am speaking my truth. I feel free from others' definitions and perceptions of me. Today and every day I listen and speak from my truth, no one else's. I live a life aligned to my most authentic desires. I do all things with honesty.*

Letters to Write to Yourself When Healing the Throat

What are the lies I tell myself? What are other people's realities and expectations that I have adopted as my own? What words do I use that reinforce false realities of myself? What is my truth? How do I want to perceive life? Where is my voice, and what other voices are covering it up? Am I ready and willing to live authentically no matter how vulnerable I have to become to do it?

When I write letters of authenticity, I address them to myself. These are the hardest to write because I have become the queen of ignoring my own needs. Being vulnerable with myself is just as hard for me as being vulnerable with another person. I created a persona of strength because my true strength was stripped from me. So when I became powerless, I began to pretend.

> *Stefani, the only peace you need to keep is your own. Allow your truth to be heard from the inside out. Your truth may change, and that is okay. Each step of your journey presents new opportunities to discover your truth. The more you reveal to yourself, the more you will receive, and in turn, the freer you will become. Today, I allow the right words in the right moment to be spoken for the highest good. Give fear and hesitation over and allow source truth to stream through. Let your voice soar through the waves of time and create a future of authenticity and joy. I am living my honesty every day.*

Affirmations for Throat Chakra Energy Work

I speak truth and unconditional authenticity!

I listen to each day with fierce honesty!

Recipes for Throat Chakra Energy Work

For each tea blend, I use loose-leaf herbs and tea leaves and make the blends in 20-ounce Mason jars. I use about ⅓ of a cup for each ingredient. I gently roll the Mason jar to mix the ingredients together without breaking up the herbs into dust.

When I'm ready to brew the tea, I heat up water in a teapot and scoop a tablespoon of the blend into a reusable tea bag. I then add my tea bag plus other ingredients such as honey or lemon (to taste) to a mug before the water is done. When the water is hot, I add it to the mug slowly.

To activate the tea with the incantation, I do a few things: First, I will write the incantation onto a sticky note and put it on the pot as it heats the water. As I pour the water slowly, I will read the incantation out loud. I stop the pour with enough room at the top of my mug so that the next part does not cause the water to spill out. Once the water is a little cooled down, I will place my right hand over the top of the mug and grasp it (not by its handle but by the rim) so that the energy from my hand is also infused into the water. Once I have a firm grip, I will pick it up and swirl the mug and tea clockwise three times while saying the incantation. I will also repeat this on my left side three times but counterclockwise. Then I will go back to my right hand and repeat the swirl but counterclockwise then left hand clockwise.

Your tea is now fully infused with the energy you intend, and once it is cooled down enough to drink, enjoy.

Authentici-Tea and Incantation

- Lavender, honey, lemon, butterfly pea, eucalyptus, full moon water

"Breaking free from the mold they made of me. Singing from the joy of authenticity. Loud and proud, there is no stopping me."

Honest-Tea and Incantation

- Peppermint, honey, butterfly pea, yerba maté, ginkgo biloba, full moon water

"Today I keep the peace within my soul. Out with the truth, breaking the mold. Keeping alignment with my soul, honesty and freedom spoken out loud."

Movement and Yoga Sequence for the Throat

Balancing and opening your throat chakra can be done differently every day; sometimes just screaming is a movement for the throat. Breath of fire practice is a very good way to start movement within the throat chakra; however, there are a few instances when people should not practice the breath of fire. You may want to make sure you do not fall into that category.

Breath of fire is calming and can cleanse and detox the diaphragm and lungs. It gets the blood flowing and circulating through the body. This is a great practice to start your day with. It will wake up your brain and set the tone for the day.

Sit comfortably on the floor or in a chair and breathe in deeply through your nose. As you breathe out, draw your lower belly inward and forcefully breathe out of your nose in quick spurts. Allow your breath to naturally fill your lungs again. Repeat this for twenty breaths, with calm inhales between each round. You can repeat this up to two more times, but it is not recommended to do more than that. The full-body yoga sequence that you could do as well is:

1. **Sun Salutation (Surya Namaskar):**
   - Start in mountain pose (tadasana) with your feet together and palms at your heart center.
   - Inhale, raise your arms overhead, and gently arch back (upward salute / urdhva hastasana).
   - Exhale, fold forward from your hips (forward fold / uttanasana), bending your knees if needed.
   - Inhale, lengthen your spine, and lift your chest halfway (halfway lift / ardha uttanasana).
   - Exhale, step or jump back into plank pose, aligning your wrists under your shoulders.
   - Lower your body halfway down with bent elbows (chaturanga dandasana).
   - Inhale, lift your chest, and gaze upward, coming into upward-facing dog (urdhva mukha svanasana).
   - Exhale, lift your hips, and press back into downward-facing dog (adho mukha svanasana).
   - Hold for a few breaths, then step or jump your feet between your hands.
   - Inhale, lift your chest halfway (halfway lift / ardha uttanasana).
   - Exhale, fold forward (forward fold / uttanasana).
   - Inhale, sweep your arms out to the sides, and come up, reaching overhead (upward salute / urdhva hastasana).

- Exhale, bring your palms together at your heart center (mountain pose/tadasana).

2. **Cat/Cow Pose (Marjaryasana/Bitilasana):**
   - Come onto all fours with your hands under your shoulders and knees under your hips.
   - Inhale, drop your belly, lift your chest, and look upward (cow pose/bitilasana).
   - Exhale, round your spine, tuck your chin toward your chest, and engage your core (cat pose/marjaryasana).
   - Flow between these two poses with your breath, moving with a gentle and fluid motion.
   - Continue for several rounds, focusing on the movement of your spine.

3. **Lion Pose (Simhasana):**
   - Kneel on the mat with your knees hip-width apart.
   - Place your hands on your thighs, spreading your fingers wide.
   - Inhale deeply through your nose.
   - Exhale forcefully, sticking your tongue out, opening your eyes wide, and roaring like a lion.
   - Repeat this breath and expression a few times, releasing tension and energizing your body.

4. **Child's Pose (Balasana):**
   - From all fours, bring your big toes together and sit back on your heels.
   - Exhale, lower your torso down, and rest your forehead on the mat.

- Extend your arms forward or rest them by your sides.
- Allow your body to relax completely, surrendering to the pose.
- Stay in this pose for a few breaths, focusing on deep relaxation.

5. **Fish Pose (Matsyasana):**
   - Lie flat on your back with your legs extended.
   - Place your hands, palms down, underneath your hips.
   - Inhale, press your forearms and elbows into the ground, lifting your chest up.
   - Arch your back, lifting your heart toward the ceiling.
   - Optional: Drop your head back gently, allowing the crown of your head to rest on the mat.
   - Hold the pose for a few breaths, feeling a gentle stretch in your chest and throat.

6. **Bridge Pose (Setu Bandha Sarvangasana):**
   - Lie flat on your back with your knees bent and feet hip-width apart.
   - Place your arms alongside your body, palms facing down.
   - Inhale, press your feet into the ground, engaging your glutes and lifting your hips off the mat.
   - Roll your shoulders back and interlace your fingers underneath your body, pressing your arms down.
   - Lengthen through your spine and lift your chest toward your chin.
   - Hold the pose for a few breaths, feeling a stretch in your chest, hips, and thighs.

7. **Plow Pose (Halasana):**

- From bridge pose, release your interlaced fingers and place your hands on your lower back for support.
- Inhale, lift your legs up and over your head, lowering your toes toward the ground behind you.
- Keep your legs straight and your core engaged.
- Optional: Support your back with your hands or keep them on the ground.
- Hold the pose for a few breaths, feeling a stretch in your back and the back of your neck.

8. **Shoulder Stand** (Salamba Sarvangasana):

- From plow pose, bend your elbows and bring your hands to your mid-back for support.
- Inhale, lift your legs up toward the ceiling, keeping them straight and together.
- Lift your hips and lower back off the mat, coming into a vertical position.
- Support your back with your hands and extend your legs upward.
- Engage your core and relax your neck.
- Hold the pose for a few breaths, feeling a gentle inversion and strengthening your upper body.

9. **Corpse Pose** (Savasana):

- Lie flat on your back with your legs extended and arms by your sides.
- Close your eyes and let go of any tension in your body.
- Relax your entire body and surrender to the pose.

- Stay in this pose for several minutes, focusing on deep rest and rejuvenation.

Remember to listen to your body and modify the poses as needed. If you're new to yoga or have any specific concerns, it's a good idea to seek guidance from a qualified yoga instructor. Enjoy your practice!

Meditations

Start with the centering and grounding meditation, open up the soul star above your head, visualize the light moving through your body touching each area of the body opening the chakras and grounding into Gaia. Remember to bring the celestial healing light and the healing earth energy up and around your extended aura. This time you are not going to travel to a guided space. You are just going to sit in the energy and prepare to do a chanting meditation.

Chant Meditation

This is a very intimidating practice for a lot of people. Even sitting alone in your house trying to chant can bring up a lot of emotions. I recommend listening to any type of repeated chant on any streaming platform and chant along with the music in order to start getting comfortable hearing your own voice. However, I wouldn't recommend staying with this; eventually listen to only instrumentals in order to really allow your own voice to be heard and exercised. The point of this meditation is to allow yourself to be heard. This practice will teach you to relax your thoughts and find just the vibration of your voice to match the frequency of the chant you are trying to produce. Letting go of the fear of "Do I sound okay and am I in tune?" to just go with the flow and sit in the vibration is very liberating.

You can find any chant, but I recommend starting with an om chant. It is simple and will open your voice to more sounds eventually. Listening to an om chant is a powerful experience all on its own, but when you are doing the chant, creating the sound and vibration from your own voice, it is even more elevating. Om or aum (ahhh-oooh-mmmm) is a sound used in the spiritual traditions of yoga and Buddhism. This sound is an uninterrupted vibration that begins deep in the throat and is continued by vibrating the vocal cords. This sound is considered the most basic of primordial sounds and the sound of the universe. Follow the steps below when you are ready to begin your practice.

1. **Find a comfortable posture:**
   - Sit in a comfortable seated position, such as cross-legged on a cushion or mat.
   - Keep your spine straight and your shoulders relaxed.
   - Rest your hands on your knees or in a comfortable mudra, such as gyan mudra (index finger and thumb touching).

2. **Relax and center yourself:**
   - Take a few deep breaths to relax your body and mind.
   - Close your eyes or maintain a soft gaze.

3. **Deep inhalation:**
   - Take a deep inhalation through your nose, filling your lungs completely.
   - Allow your breath to be smooth and natural.

4. **Exhalation with "oh" sound:**

   • On the exhalation, slowly begin to chant the sound "oh" (pronounced like "aum" or "om").

   • Let the sound emerge from deep within your abdomen and resonate in your chest.

   • Draw out the sound of "oh" for the entire duration of your exhalation.

   • Focus on the vibration and resonance of the sound as you chant.

5. **Continue chanting:**

   • Inhale deeply again and repeat the chant of "oh" on the exhalation.

   • Allow the sound to be continuous and steady.

   • Maintain a relaxed and effortless flow of breath and sound.

6. **Connect with the vibrations:**

   • As you chant, feel the vibrations of the sound throughout your body.

   • Be aware of the sound resonating in your throat, chest, and even in the space around you.

   • Embrace the sense of unity and connection that the sound of "om" brings.

7. **Set your intention:**

   • As you continue chanting, you can silently set an intention or focus your mind on a particular purpose.

   • It can be a personal intention, gratitude, peace, or any positive quality you wish to cultivate.

8. **Chant for a few minutes:**
   - Repeat the chanting of "om" for a few minutes, allowing yourself to fully immerse in the experience.
   - Let go of any expectations and simply surrender to the practice.

9. **Gradual conclusion:**
   - When you are ready to conclude the chanting, gradually allow the sound to fade away.
   - Take a few moments of silence to observe the residual vibrations and sensations in your body and mind.

Chanting "om" can be a deeply personal and meditative experience. It is not only a sound but also a sacred symbol representing the unity of all things. This practice will most certainly create a connection to universal source energy.

The Throat Activation

Both of the exercises mentioned already (the meditation and the yoga practice) will activate and heal the throat, but not everyone is going to do yoga or chant. There are many other ways to work with the throat besides the tools already mentioned. A few simpler ways, which I'm sure you can already guess, would be to sing, but try to sing without music. Sing to the person that you need to speak your truth to. Sing to yourself all the hard things you need to hear; make it up as you go. Look in the mirror and make a fun game of it; act it out in a musical, dramatically expressing yourself to whoever needs to hear what you have to say. Talk to yourself as the interviewee and interviewer. Ask yourself all the hard questions out loud and allow yourself to keep talking through your excuses until you get to the core truth. And remember, all of this is out loud.

I think everyone's favorite would be screaming in the car when no one is around, except try to scream a sentence. Let yourself be angry if that is where you're at and say all the mean, unhinged things that are stuck. This will get you to the next level of truth. Don't deny the raw emotions even if they aren't the full scope of your truth; just express them. Practice saying your boundaries out loud as well. Say them with authority and strength. Take an improv or acting class or go to an open mic, storytelling, comedy, or poetry event and just let yourself be heard no matter what comes out. Remember, this is just the activation, not the actual expression.

The next part is my favorite. After I have activated my throat, no matter what the situation, who I need to say it to, or what needs to be said, I always say, "Please provide me with the right words at the right time for my truth to be heard." You can speak this to the universe, to God, to source energy, or to anyone or anything that you know is guiding you. This is not just for your ability to speak your truth but for your truth to be heard so you are not on an endless wheel.

Ritual

The ritual for the throat chakra is all about authenticity and honesty. Using the throat chakra in order to manifest is a very powerful way to get exactly what you want. Of course, be selective who you say things out loud to. As with anything in life, you need to know your audience. What are the intentions and energies of the people you are giving your truth to? The more you work with your own energy centers and do your shadow work, the more you will be able to see each individual's energy.

Finding Your Voice

First, write down what you want to bring into your life. Make a list of all the things you want, but the trick is to write with love and gratitude and not overwhelm yourself. You want it to be in bite-size chunks because you are going to say them out loud every single day until you are exactly where you want to be. Here is an example list of what you may want and how you will want to write it:

1. I am grateful for the money I make every week, more than enough to pay for all the bills.
2. I am grateful money flows to me every single day.
3. I am grateful for the beautiful house I live in.
4. I am grateful for how successful I am with my creative endeavors and all the people who buy my work.
5. I am in love with my ability to create every day.
6. I am in love with my friends and the community of people I interact with every day.
7. I am in love with my healing and growth and continued options in life.
8. I am grateful I know all the right ways to treat my body to stay active and healthy.
9. I am in love with and grateful for the joy and connection I have with my partner and children.
10. I am in love with and grateful for my freedom!

Write all the things that you want to create in your life—body, mind, and soul—and say them out loud until you feel these are all present in your life. You can always change and refine each one. It's about changing the way you feel about your reality, and then your reality will show up for you. I often say them out loud while I am out for a walk listening to music that makes my heart happy, giving myself an extra boost of *hell yeah, this is my life!* This will truly create that new awareness in your reticular activating system, and you will begin to see everything was always already there for you.

Psychic Center of the Throat

There are actually three psychic centers that become activated when you have a clear and open throat channel: clairgustance, clear taste; clairalience, clear smelling; and clairaudience, clear hearing.

Clairgustance

This is the rare gift of having a taste show up as guidance from spirit. Some will suddenly experience a bad or bitter taste when the spirit is trying to tell them they are headed in the wrong direction. You can also experience the opposite, a sudden sweet taste to give you validation. Some may even experience the taste of something a loved one used to make when they were alive to indicate their presence.

Clairalience

Similar to clairgustance is clairalience, when you smell something that isn't actually present to indicate a loved one or a spirit guide with certain scent associations is around. For example, smelling roses suddenly could indicate Mary is around you. A common scent that shows up when this ability is developed is when you had a loved one who smoked and all of a sudden you smell cigarettes, but no one is currently smoking around you. You may also smell cologne or perfume that you haven't smelled since they were alive. Both of these are connected to a clear throat chakra channel. However, so is the ability to hear.

Clairaudience

Clairaudience is the most common of the three and also the one that gives us the most information when we learn to listen. We will focus on refining our clairaudience through automatic writing. This is a practice that, like all others, takes time to master but is very effective once you have. Be patient with yourself and allow your ego to filter out as you go.

Choose a time when you will have no distractions and a space, preferably an altar or table that you do divination at and already have intention energy connected to. You can use pen and paper or type. The tools here are less important than the act of doing the writing; however, I would use the same notebook or open document each time you practice. Set up your energy to be in a meditative state before you begin. You can use the centering and grounding visualization that we've been using throughout the book or simply use other tools such as incense or music to activate the energy.

You will focus on a question you or someone else has, and you will write it down on paper. Then you will begin to write. Filter out your ego first. If you need to write things like, "I'm not sure how to answer this," "What should my pen be doing?" "How will I know if it is real?" Then answer those first: "Trust the process," "Trust your voice," "You will gain clarity and find what you are looking for." Give yourself that extra reinforcement if you need to, then go back to the original question.

You can also start here with your own voice, but eventually let it taper off to allow automatic writing to begin. Allow your voice to be positive by giving yourself encouragement through your words. Before you know it, you will start to feel as if there is a truth coming through as you write, and you will surrender to that truth. Eventually, you will be writing without ego. You'll feel that the message is complete when the writing stops. It feels like the energy has just turned off. Some people suggest you do not look at the paper or screen when you are writing. This can be good for you to free yourself of your consciousness. You may also find that you can look but your eyes take more of a psychic gaze. Your mind will not truly be registering what it is you are writing.

Chapter Seven
Third Eye Chakra, Ajna

The third eye is energetically located in the center of the forehead. This energy center's activations, and the visualizations, will mostly take place in this location; however, the pineal gland in the center of the mind is the muscle of this energy center. It's the part of the mind that we expand and connect to infinite wisdom. In this section, you will read about opening, cleansing, and expanding both areas of the mind. This energy center is easily fragmented. Being fragmented in the wrong way can lead to mental health disorders. However, learning to hear the mind in separation—the different parts such as the chatter of our past, the connection to the higher realm, and the thoughts of others—while remaining whole within your own neurological pathways can lead to deep psychic and metaphysical experiences. It is important to take time to practice oneness with yourself through each of the chakras before trying to develop the different skills within the mind.

We can work in this energy center with all the different psychic abilities, such as clairvoyance, which I will get into later, but we can also begin to learn astral projection, telepathy, remote viewing, and dreamwalking from this energy center. It is very important to be actively working with your shadow side and questioning your growth and progress when dealing with the third eye and even later when we get to the crown. This is a journey you will want to go on with a community of like-minded people. You can find these people through online communities already available or create your own. When working with the third eye, you should treat it as a book study—constantly learning and evolving with new frequencies and information. I learn every day from people going through their awakening for the first time and from the OGs of spiritual enlightenment. There will never be a shortage of new information and experiences to be had.

Both the third eye and the pineal gland generate portals to information that is already occurring. It may be occurring in a parallel alignment or in a current reality. You can even open portals to information that has already taken place and has energetic footprints to it. These two sources, pineal gland and third eye together, can tap into an infinite amount of information. These infinite energies of information can come through in so many forms: telepathy, past lives, soul mates, soul babies, medical intuition (being able to see discord or disease in the body), cords between people, and so much more. I like to think of it like the hypothetical mycelium between us that we have forgotten about, energetic pathways that we can learn to tap into once again. Our third eye and pineal gland have been corroded by energetic pollution as well as environmental pollution, but our natural state of function has the ability to do all of these things.

When your third eye is clear and balanced, you will be able to make decisions from an emotionally detached place, trusting your own foresight and intuition. When your third eye is blocked or not in balance, you will have a hard time making decisions. When it is fragmented, you will have poor memory recall. When your third eye is overactive, you will have a difficult time with current reality and will be living in fantasy. You may not be able to ground either.

I See

The affirmation "I see" reflects the intuitive and perceptive qualities of this chakra. It emphasizes the capacity to gain insight, trust one's inner wisdom, and see things on a deeper level, both physically and spiritually. A clear, balanced third eye not only allows you to see the visions beyond the current moment; it also enables trust within those visions. I see with clear vision the patterns of each decision and reality. I see with clear vision what a shift in perspective and behavior will achieve, and I trust in the clarity.

Tools and Properties of the Third Eye for Alignment

Emotional connections: Calm, focused, constant flow of ideas, joy or depression, restful sleep, nightmares, bigger-picture oriented, ability to see life's connections, feeling empowered, perceptions, idealism

Physical connections: The senses, the eyes, ears, nose, forehead, brain, sinus passageways, cheeks, pineal gland

Foods: Eggplant, purple cabbage, blackberries, purple potatoes, purple kale, purple carrots

Activities: Reading fiction and nonfiction to activate visualization

Color: Purple—The third eye responds to purple color therapy and balances when fed purple foods.

Element: All five elements are present in the third eye, or we can say the element is light.

Tones and Notes: A, om—Listening to music, sounds, and frequencies that have these in them can break up blocks and clear out energy in the third eye. Chanting the sound om is very effective. In addition to activating the throat, it aids in healing. Practicing or listening to this chant can be a very healing tool

for anyone to use. Attend a sound healing class or listen to frequencies on any music app.

Gemstones

Gemstones have many uses for healing and vibrational alignment.
They are widely used in holistic practices among many cultures.
If you choose to work on one chakra at a time the way this book
is laid out, you may want to wear gemstones as jewelry to create
a vibrational frequency that aligns to the energy you are moving
through. However, you can use them during meditation either on
an altar or placed upon the chakra you are working with. You may
want to set a routine for this type of meditation or for when you
are in the middle of experiencing the emotions. Setting multiple
gemstones together around the house in a patterned grid amplifies
the energy you are working with and creates movement of this
energy. You can do this during the entire cycle of working with this
chakra, then change the grid when you move to the next chakra.

> *Lapis lazuli:* This stone enhances one's intuition and con-
> nects them to their inner wisdom. It can help individ-
> uals access deeper levels of consciousness, promoting
> self-awareness. Lapis lazuli is often associated with spiri-
> tual growth and enlightenment. It is said to stimulate the
> higher mind and expand one's awareness, allowing for a
> deeper understanding of spiritual truths and universal
> concepts. It also provides spiritual protection and shields
> the aura from negative energies. It is often used to ward
> off psychic attacks, promote energetic balance, and create
> a sense of spiritual harmony. This is a popular stone for
> meditation and spiritual practices. Its calming energy and
> ability to stimulate the third eye chakra can aid in deep-

ening meditation experiences, accessing higher states of consciousness, and connecting with spiritual guides or higher realms. Lapis lazuli assists in emotional healing by bringing deep-seated emotions to the surface for release and transformation. It can help alleviate stress, anxiety, and depression while promoting inner peace and serenity. Lapis lazuli has long been associated with spiritual and divine connections. It is believed to facilitate a stronger connection to one's higher self as well as to spiritual guides, angels, and other celestial beings.

Labradorite: It is believed to help individuals navigate through transitions and challenges in life, providing inner strength and resilience during times of upheaval. Labradorite is often referred to as the stone of magic due to its association with enhancing intuition and psychic abilities. It is believed to open the third eye chakra and stimulate spiritual awareness, allowing for clearer insights, intuitive guidance, and a deeper connection to higher realms. It is also thought to have powerful protective properties, creating a shield against negative energies, psychic attacks, and unwanted influences. It is believed to help balance and strengthen the aura, preventing energy leaks and promoting energetic harmony. Labradorite is associated with expanding one's consciousness and spiritual growth. It is believed to facilitate access to spiritual dimensions and past-life memories. It can aid in deepening meditation practices and connecting with spiritual guides and higher wisdom. Labradorite has a harmonizing effect on the body, mind, and spirit. It is thought to balance and align the chakras, promoting overall energetic equilibrium and a sense of well-being. It may also help to integrate spiritual and earthly energies.

Dumortierite: This stone helps individuals develop their psychic senses, such as clairvoyance and clairaudience. Dumortierite organizes thoughts, improves concentration, and enhances mental abilities. It is often used to clear mental fog, stimulate intellectual pursuits, and support decision-making processes. Dumortierite assists individuals in exploring their true selves, uncovering hidden talents, and expanding their spiritual awareness. Dumortierite is also good for the throat chakra to help individuals articulate their thoughts and emotions with clarity and confidence. Dumortierite is often used to improve public speaking skills, facilitate effective communication in relationships, and support creative expression.

Iolite: This stone enhances the awakening and activation of the third eye, facilitating psychic abilities, intuition, and inner vision. Iolite facilitates the exploration of one's true purpose and path in life. It sharpens the mind, stimulates intuitive insights, and strengthens the connection with higher realms and spiritual guidance.

Amethyst: Referred to as the stone of spiritual awakening, it assists in opening and activating the third eye and crown chakras, facilitating a deeper connection with higher realms and spiritual insights. Amethyst helps individuals develop their psychic senses, such as clairvoyance and clairaudience, and strengthen their connection to their higher self and spiritual guides. Amethyst assists in receiving and interpreting spiritual messages and insights, fostering a deeper understanding of one's life purpose and spiritual path.

Celestite: It is called the stone of angels due to its strong connection to angelic realms. It facilitates communication with angels, spirit guides, and higher beings. Celestite can help individuals receive divine guidance, wisdom, and support from the spiritual realm. It assists in quieting the mind, promoting clear thinking, and improving communication skills. Celestite assists individuals in gaining spiritual insights, deepening their connection to higher realms, and fostering spiritual growth. Celestite is often used in spiritual practices to raise vibrational frequency and expand awareness.

Oils and Herbs

As with gemstones, oils and herbs can be used in many ways during the healing process. I like to use these specifically during difficult times while working through each energy field. Not only can you experience moments of intense emotion, you may also experience what's called a healing crisis. Sometimes during a healing crisis it can feel like you have flu-like symptoms. This is actually the toxins leaving the body. You can experience this after a reiki session or sometimes after a yoga sequence. There are other times you may experience a healing crisis, and in these instances, I find it useful to use the oils and herbs. This is also a good time to drink the tea blends.

Frankincense: Its aroma is believed to induce a state of calm, focus, and mental clarity, facilitating a deeper connection with one's inner self and the spiritual realms. Frankincense is often associated with the expansion of consciousness and spiritual awakening. It is believed to elevate the vibrational frequency and help individuals access higher states of awareness, wisdom, and spiritual insights. It is believed to calm the mind, relieve stress, and promote emotional healing. Frankincense's energy can help individuals find inner peace, balance their emotions, and release emotional blockages. It is believed to facilitate communication with spiritual beings, guides, and ascended masters. Frankincense is often used to invoke blessings, seek guidance, and deepen one's spiritual connection.

Peppermint: Known for its invigorating and stimulating properties, it can help clear the mind, improve concentration, and enhance mental clarity. Peppermint is often used during meditation or spiritual practices to promote alertness and focus. It has a refreshing and uplifting energy. It can help revitalize the spirit, boost energy levels, and promote a sense of vitality. Peppermint helps individuals tune in to their inner guidance, heighten their intuitive abilities, and deepen their spiritual connection. Peppermint is known for its uplifting and mood-enhancing effects. It can help alleviate feelings of sadness, stress, or anxiety, promoting a more positive and joyful state of mind. Peppermint is often used as a natural mood booster and emotional support. Peppermint is sometimes associated with spiritual purification and connection to the Divine. It is believed to aid in spiritual growth and exploration.

Marjoram: This herb creates a protective energy field around individuals, shielding them from negative influences, psychic attacks, and energetic disturbances. Marjoram assists individuals in attuning to higher frequencies and receiving divine guidance. It is often used in meditation or spiritual practices to deepen one's connection to the Divine and access spiritual insights. Marjoram deepens the connection with the subconscious mind. It assists individuals in recalling dreams, accessing insights from the dream realm, and enhancing spiritual growth through dream exploration. Marjoram is often used as an herbal infusion before bedtime to support dream experiences.

Lavender: This herb has a calming and balancing energy that can help individuals quiet the mind, open their senses, and tap into their intuitive insights. Lavender helps individuals expand their awareness, access spiritual insights, and deepen their connection to the Divine. Lavender has relaxing properties that can support restful sleep and aid in dream recall. Lavender is often used in pillows, sachets, or as a mist on bedding to promote a peaceful sleep environment and facilitate dream experiences.

Valerian: This herb helps calm the mind, reduce anxiety, and ease stress, allowing individuals to achieve a state of tranquility conducive to meditation, prayer, or spiritual connection. Valerian is used to promote vivid, lucid dreaming. It opens the channels of communication with the subconscious mind and the spiritual realm, facilitating the exploration of the dream world and spiritual insights that may arise during sleep. Valerian helps individuals enter a receptive state that is conducive to spiritual practices such as meditation, divination, or energy healing. It is believed to heighten sensitivity and attunement to spiritual energies.

Chamomile: This plant has a gentle and calming energy that can help quiet the mind, reduce anxiety, and bring about a state of tranquility conducive to meditation, prayer, or spiritual connection. Chamomile opens the channels of perception and promotes a clearer connection with higher realms of consciousness. Chamomile may be used to facilitate intuitive insights, enhance divination practices, and strengthen spiritual awareness. Chamomile has a reputation for promoting restful sleep and vivid dreams. In spiritual practices, it is often used to support dream work and enhance dream experiences. Chamomile is believed to facilitate communication with the subconscious mind and the spiritual realm during sleep, promoting spiritual insights and guidance through dreams.

Basil: This is a sacred herb in certain spiritual traditions and deepens one's spiritual practice. Basil is sometimes used in meditation, prayer, or ritual ceremonies to facilitate a stronger connection with the Divine, higher realms, or one's inner self.

Shadow Work

The following practice is the flow I like to use when doing my own shadow work. There is no wrong way. Find what works for you and move at your own pace.

1. Where are your physical issues? If you have stomach issues, maybe start with the solar plexus. If you are not sure about what is physically out of alignment, I would simply start with the root and move up from there.

2. Once you decide which chakra you are going to start focusing on, put your energy and thoughts toward that chakra at night. Even before knowing what may come up, simply put your hands on that energy center as you

fall asleep. You can send healing light visually to that chakra and say out loud or to yourself "I am ready to release any stuck and unhealed energy. I am ready to see what has been hiding in the shadows." Then be open to what happens next. Your days to follow will bring up issues you have been avoiding.

3. Set time aside weekly for processing the emotions, emotional reactions, triggers, and social interactions that are coming up. You may even want to do this daily before you go to bed. Start journaling the questions you are asking and answering for yourself.

4. Finally, decide which of the provided tools you will use and create a routine for each. Slowly integrate changes into your routine. Do not try to do everything all at once. In order to create sustainable lifestyle changes, you should start with one at a time. After you feel comfortable with steps two and three, maybe add drinking herbal teas or yoga once a week.

Questions for Third Eye Chakra Shadow Work

Shadow work for this energy center is going to look a little different. We are dealing with a very powerful muscle when talking about the third eye. We have to combine it with the mind and not get caught in the separation of the two. The questions that you have to ask yourself might feel like a self-diagnosis of some sort, and I recommend lots of feedback when working on healing the mind. You could use a therapist, a life coach, a reiki master, or a professional of your choice. Friends and books are also great for this work, but you may want a little more support. You are not actually trying to find a diagnosis. You are seeking to understand patterns of the mind and how they commonly occur in order to filter them from your recycled energy and create new patterns.

When I got to my shadow work of the third eye and mind, I was diagnosed with ADHD. This was at forty-two years old. I did not start taking medication after all those years for this diagnosis, but it did help me see clearly what were impulses created by this type of brain activity and what were truths being spoken in my body, mind, and soul. It helped me hear the different parts of myself more clearly. If I hadn't realized the patterns of my mind, I may have continued to swim lost without direction.

I believe that the mind's shadow work is where we gain the map to our consciousness. It is where we can learn to overcome our hamster wheel of recurring internal and external circumstances. We can start to see our ego and our soul as two separate yet equally important pieces of our human reality. Often in spiritual practices, we are taught to overcome the ego, release it, and let it go. This step is even more important to living a full life of joy and laughter. Without knowing the parts of my thoughts that come from trauma, ADHD, psychic abilities, and other people's opinions, I would never know how to find myself.

It is crucial that you seek information when working on the mind. Finding spiritual books doesn't stop with one spiritual belief. Oftentimes people find something that feels good—Christianity, Buddhism, and such—and stay with that course of enlightenment. However, that is not how you learn about your whole mind; you only learn about a portion. Read it all: the Bible, the Rig Veda, the sutras—as much as you can. They are all branches of the heart that others have interpreted for you. Ask yourself, what are some of your patterns of the mind that align with these spiritual beliefs? Read psychology books, metaphysical books, books from gurus and coaches. Find pieces of you in all of them. Then talk about what you have read and create new patterns, actually do things differently. You will start to notice here in the mind and third eye most of the other chakra energies you have worked on will be present.

You may want to revisit some of the questions you asked yourself while working with the previous chakras: Who am I? What are my beliefs, desires, and goals? Where is my passion, my strength, my courage? What makes me feel loved, and where is my truth? Where is my voice? These questions and more will show up again. This time you are looking at them as energies that have predicted thought patterns and actions. You look for what you know. Your brain registers the world around you based on what you can already identify. So in order to do this shadow work, you have to work on new identifications. You have to receive new information in order to open up to new possibilities.

Ask yourself, What are you holding onto? What do you constantly see showing up in your life? This one is hard for some people because we don't want to believe that the world shows up according to how we show up. How would you describe your dating experiences and relationships? How do you handle interactions with individuals who display anger or frustration in the service industry? How do you generally experience and cope with feelings of frustration in your daily life? Of course, sometimes we get thrown curve balls, but we pivot and adjust in the same way we show up. It can lead to new adventures, or it can lead to more frustration and stuck energy. After a certain age, when we become in control of our choices, it is up to us to choose how we see life. I understand the argument that bad things and horrible things are occurring around us every day. However, we choose to engage in those things at our level of capability. The bomb didn't go off without years and even generations of misalignment. I believe that if we taught every seven-year-old to meditate, in one hundred years we would be looking at a very peaceful world. I don't believe the best course of action is to engage in the war once they have already begun to fight. We need to change the way we see ourselves long before we get to that point.

We want to think about the reticular activating system (RAS) again and its complex network of neurons located in the brainstem. The RAS acts as a gatekeeper for sensory information, filtering out irrelevant or unimportant stimuli while allowing significant or novel stimuli to reach conscious awareness. This filtering process helps prevent sensory overload and allows the brain to focus on the most relevant information.

Why is this important in *Chakras and Shadow Work*? You need new information to start to begin to see and show up differently. If all you see is pain and despair, you need to open up to the love and joy in life and start to see that. I heard it explained like this once: at any given moment, every song ever created is playing; however, we only hear the ones we know or choose to listen to. You can tap into the waves of the music playing once you are aware they are playing.

Mirror neurons (for the purpose of this book) are the second part of discovering your mind and learning how to train or retrain it. Mirror neurons may be the culprits of keeping us on the hamster wheel. As was already mentioned they, are exactly what they sound like. They are the part of the brain that mirrors the things you see. I was fascinated when I first learned about mirror neurons because it explained why my mouth would start chewing when I was talking to someone who had gum in their mouth or why my foot would kick when I was watching soccer. Mirror neurons are responsible for the "monkey see, monkey do" part of our brain that is quite real. This is why every success coach has been saying for years to surround yourself with people who are successful and that you start to become who you hang out with.

These neurons not only make you feel the feelings of those around you, they open up your RAS to new possibilities and you start to become and act "as if." The shadow work here is all about taking responsibility for your environment. What are you surrounding yourself with? We can ask ourselves, what are we attracting? The reality is, we attract what we know over and over again. This is why it is crucial to seek new information, get out of our comfort zone, and be an active participant in our manifestations.

There are so many parts to understanding the mind. It's the most fascinating, crucial part of all this work. First, understand the patterns that you've created for yourself based on survival instincts. Second, discover your patterns based on special ways your mind receives and processes information. Third, seek new information and put yourself in new situations. Open up to the idea that anything is possible. This work can only be done when you are ready. It is extremely hard to see life from the exciting possibility of going into the unknown. However, once you are there and you are ready, you will begin to experience the "spiritual awakening" everyone talks about, because you will see the world in a completely new way, and you will never be able to unsee it.

Once you get to this part of your journey, you will start to see new experiences that you never saw before. People will show up in your life to offer you these experiences. Conversations will show up that are new, and the people around you will start to change. You may not be able to relate to the people you once held close to you. This can be a very intense part of your journey, but it can also be the most exciting. You will start to experience your mind in a way that you never thought possible. You will be able to feel the differences between your ego and other people's minds. We will explore what that actually feels like in the upcoming meditation, The Third Eye Activation. This is the work where you listen and then listen some more. You allow your mind to stop the repetition and expand or zoom out. You begin to see the world around you very differently than you have ever seen it before.

While writing this section, I went back to New York. I hadn't been back to see my friends that I grew up with in five years. The city looked and felt completely different. I couldn't even conjure up the feeling I had when I was in my twenties enjoying the adventures Lower Manhattan had to offer. It was a completely new experience, as if I didn't spend every year of my life before my first Saturn return in that state. I did not grieve this change or view it as a loss of nostalgia; I openly embraced it with a smile and allowed myself to feel like I was on vacation, like I might feel in any other country or state I had never been to before. I had conversations with people I had known for forty years and listened to their new perspectives on life as if it were the first time we had ever sat at the table together.

This is such a vital experience of doing shadow work. Everyone sees life very differently from their lens of experiences. We perceive life from what we have already gathered and become familiar with. So listening to the experiences of others can open your understanding differently than books or even living them yourself can. This is because it is one sided in that you're only experiencing your emotions, not truly experiencing the emotions of others. This is extremely important if you identify as an empath. As an empath, you can feel what others are feeling if they are actively in the feeling, projecting the feeling, or simply recalling the feeling. Feelings create the movement of our energy.

Let me explain it like this: I was telling two very different people a story about my recent adventures. One of these people viewed my adventures as seeking validation while the other viewed them as a celebration of self. Either one of those stories I could have attached to and questioned my own reality. People will always give their opinions no matter what you are sharing. It is not conducive to a life full of joy to just avoid everyone in order to avoid those that see your adventures as "seeking validation" because you'll miss out on the people who see your adventures as "a celebration of self." However, you must have enough experience in expanding your mind in order to not attach to the one that doesn't keep your energy in motion toward the vibes you are trying to create in your life. In order to seek out and attract more of that, you have to learn how to sift, pivot, cope, and follow the green flags.

Letter for Third Eye Chakra Shadow Work

This is good to do at any time; however, if you want to enhance the energy around your letter and intentions, pay attention to what planets are in what zodiac sign. You can align your intentions with the energy that is strongest during that time. Here's an example:

Venus in Leo. Show up as yourself! Fiercely love yourself and look for others who celebrate with you! You'll be shown which way to move when your eyes and mind are all the way open.

Letters to Write to Yourself When Healing the Third Eye Chakra

If I could see all possibilities, which would I choose to see?

Dear me, I am more than I see at the moment, and I look for the parts of me in everything that shows up around me. I will move toward the parts of me that bring me joy and peace. I know that the way I see the world is a result of my past experiences, and if I want to change my external reality, I have to do things differently and move out of my comfort zone. Working from what I already know will only produce what it has already produced. I am showing up as my true, authentic self and making adjustments as needed to move toward the creation of a beautiful, healthy, adventurous life.

Affirmations for Third Eye Chakra Energy Work

I see all possibilities!

I see from new eyes and an expanded mind!

I see a world that is beautiful and nourishing!

I see all things as a reflection of my own mind!

Recipes for Third Eye Chakra Energy Work

For each tea blend, I use loose-leaf herbs and tea leaves and make the blends in 20-ounce Mason jars. I use about ⅓ of a cup for each ingredient. I gently roll the Mason jar to mix the ingredients together without breaking up the herbs into dust.

When I'm ready to brew the tea, I heat up water in a teapot and scoop a tablespoon of the blend into a reusable tea bag. I then add my tea bag plus other ingredients such as honey or lemon (to taste) to a mug before the water is done. When the water is hot, I add it to the mug slowly.

To activate the tea with the incantation, I do a few things: First, I will write the incantation onto a sticky note and put it on the pot as it heats the water. As I pour the water slowly, I will read the incantation out loud. I stop the pour with enough room at the top of my mug so that the next part does not cause the water to spill out. Once the water is a little cooled down, I will place my right hand over the top of the mug and grasp it (not by its handle but by the rim) so that the energy from my hand is also infused into the water. Once I have a firm grip, I will pick it up and swirl the mug and tea clockwise three times while saying the incantation. I will also repeat this on my left side three times but counterclockwise. Then I will go back to my right hand and repeat the swirl but counterclockwise then left hand clockwise.

Your tea is now fully infused with the energy you intend, and once it is cooled down enough to drink, enjoy.

Psychic Dreams Tea and Incantation

- Valerian, lavender, chamomile, jasmine, lavender syrup

"Now I lay me down to sleep, gods and goddesses, show me secrets you keep. May I roam while my body rests at home. Before I wake, bring visions of the future for me to take."

"Silent Night" Tea and Incantation

- Lavender, rose, chamomile, new moon water, damiana

"Watching the embers, soothing the flame. The fire inside too big to tame. Simmer the pot, not too hot, drink up the potion and open the portals of motion."

Movement and Yoga Sequence for the Third Eye

Balancing and opening your third eye chakra can be done every day. Whether you simply meditate or do a movement sequence, there is always something you can do to see life more clearly. An open mind allows us to see things that were always there but that we were blind to before, as well as new pathways that may have never been there. Your visions are endless.

1. **Mountain Pose (Tadasana):**
   - Stand tall with your feet together or hip-width apart.
   - Distribute your weight evenly through the soles of your feet.
   - Lengthen your spine and relax your shoulders.
   - Engage your core muscles and keep your chin parallel to the floor.
   - Relax your arms by your sides.

2. **Forward Fold (Uttanasana):**
   - From mountain pose, exhale and hinge forward at your hips.
   - Bend your knees slightly if needed to release tension in the hamstrings.
   - Let your head and neck relax, allowing them to hang toward the ground.
   - Place your hands on the floor beside your feet or hold onto your shins.
   - Breathe deeply and relax into the pose.

3. **Downward-Facing Dog (Adho Mukha Svanasana):**
   - Start on your hands and knees, with your wrists aligned under your shoulders and knees under your hips.
   - Tuck your toes and lift your knees off the floor, straightening your legs.
   - Press your palms firmly into the mat and engage your core.
   - Lift your sitting bones toward the ceiling, creating an inverted V shape with your body.

- Keep your heels reaching toward the ground and relax your neck.

4. **Sun Salutation (Surya Namaskar):**

- Begin in mountain pose.
- Inhale, raise your arms overhead, and arch your back slightly (upward salute / urdhva hastasana).
- Exhale, fold forward into forward fold (uttanasana).
- Inhale, lift your chest, and gaze forward (halfway lift / ardha uttanasana).
- Exhale, step or jump back into a plank position.
- Lower your body down to the ground, keeping your elbows close to your sides (chaturanga dandasana).
- Inhale, press into your hands, and lift your chest for upward-facing dog (urdhva mukha svanasana) or cobra (bhujangasana).
- Exhale, lift your hips, and come into downward-facing dog (adho mukha svanasana).
- Step or jump your feet forward to forward fold (uttanasana).
- Inhale, rise up with a flat back, and reach your arms overhead (upward salute / urdhva hastasana).
- Exhale, lower your arms to your sides, and return to mountain pose.

5. **Warrior I (Virabhadrasana I):**

- From mountain pose, step your left foot back, keeping your front foot facing forward.
- Rotate your back foot slightly outward, aligning your heel with the arch of your front foot.

- Bend your front knee to a 90-degree angle, keeping it stacked over your ankle.
- Square your hips and shoulders to the front of the mat.
- Raise your arms overhead, keeping your palms facing each other or bringing them together.
- Gaze forward or up, and hold the pose while breathing deeply.

6. **Pyramid Pose (Parsvottonasana):**
   - From warrior I, square your hips forward and straighten your front leg.
   - Keep your back foot grounded, toes pointing slightly outward.
   - Hinge forward from your hips, bringing your torso toward your front leg.
   - Place your hands on the floor beside your front foot or on your shin.
   - Keep your spine lengthened and breathe deeply into the stretch.
   - Hold the pose, then repeat on the other side.

7. **Warrior III (Virabhadrasana III):**
   - From pyramid pose, shift your weight onto your right foot.
   - Hinge forward at your hips while lifting your left leg straight behind you.
   - Keep your hips and shoulders parallel to the ground.
   - Extend your arms forward or alongside your body.
   - Flex your left foot and engage your core for balance.

- Find a focal point to assist with balance and breathe steadily.

- Hold the pose, then repeat on the other side.

8. **Tree Pose (Vrikshasana):**

- Begin in warrior III.

- Shift your weight onto your left foot and place your right foot on your left inner thigh.

- Press your foot into your thigh and your thigh into your foot, finding balance.

- Bring your hands to prayer position at your heart or raise them overhead.

- Focus on a stable point in front of you and breathe deeply.

- Hold the pose, then repeat on the other side.

9. **Yogi Squat (Malasana):**

- Stand with your feet wider than hip-width apart, toes pointing slightly outward.

- Lower your body into a squat position, keeping your heels on the ground.

- Bring your palms together at your heart, pressing your elbows against your inner knees.

- Keep your spine straight and chest lifted.

- Breathe deeply and hold the pose, feeling a gentle opening in the hips and groin.

10. **Extended Child's Pose (Balasana):**

- Begin on your hands and knees in a tabletop position.

- Widen your knees and bring your big toes to touch.

- Sit your hips back toward your heels and walk your hands forward.
- Lower your forehead to the ground or rest it on a block or bolster.
- Allow your entire body to relax, focusing on deep breaths into your back.

11. **Staff Pose (Dandasana):**

- Sit on the floor with your legs extended in front of you.
- Keep your spine straight and press your sitting bones into the ground.
- Flex your feet and engage your leg muscles.
- Rest your hands on the floor beside your hips.
- Lengthen your spine and gaze forward, breathing evenly.

12. **Cow Face Pose (Gomukhasana):**

- Start in a seated position with your legs extended.
- Bend your right knee and cross your right leg over your left, placing your right foot beside your left hip.
- Bend your left knee and tuck your left foot under your right buttock.
- Stack your knees on top of each other.
- Extend your right arm overhead and bend it, reaching your right hand between your shoulder blades.
- Extend your left arm to the side and bend it, reaching your left hand up your back.
- Optional: Clasp your hands together.
- Breathe deeply and hold the pose, then switch sides.

13. **Bound Angle Pose (Baddha Konasana):**

  • Sit on the floor with your legs extended in front of you.

  • Bend your knees and bring the soles of your feet together, allowing your knees to drop out to the sides.

  • Hold onto your feet or ankles with your hands.

  • Lengthen your spine and gently press your knees toward the ground.

  • Relax your shoulders and breathe deeply into the stretch.

14. **Seated Meditation:**

  • Find a comfortable seated position, either cross-legged on the floor or on a cushion or chair.

  • Close your eyes or soften your gaze.

  • Rest your hands on your knees or in your lap.

  • Lengthen your spine, relax your shoulders, and settle into a relaxed yet alert posture.

  • Focus on your breath or a chosen point of focus.

  • Allow your thoughts to come and go without judgment, returning your attention to your breath or focal point whenever you become aware of distractions.

  • Remain in the seated meditation for the desired duration, maintaining a calm and peaceful state of mind.

Meditations

You will follow the same centering and grounding meditation that you have been practicing throughout the entire book, then we will continue past the doors of meditation. At this point of your practice, it will be much easier to turn on this meditative state. You should be at the point where you feel the act of getting into meditation is the flip of a switch.

You are about to take your practice to a deeper level, a trance-like state. Here you will begin to recognize that your visions are in no way connected to your ego or imagination. (I have noticed in my own practice that when my imagination interrupts the visions in the trance, spirit quickly dissolves that image I have placed into the vision.)

Akashic Records

Visualize white light pouring in through the top of your mind, opening and expanding your crown chakra. Allow this liquid light of healing to release all thoughts. Feel your mind become quiet and soft. Release your facial muscles, eyes, jaw.

Visualize your third eye and pineal gland opening and releasing old energy, renewed with clear sight. Let the white light pour down your spine, opening your throat chakra, relaxing your shoulders. Feel the energy slowly move down your arms, relaxing every muscle. Feel your arms soften as the energy moves past your elbows, releasing tension in your wrists and activating your palm chakras.

Feel this white light opening and healing your heart chakra, allowing your back muscles to fully relax, sinking deeper into healing. Feel the energy move down into your solar plexus, healing your organs and cleansing your body. The energy slowly moves into your sacral, activating inspiration and creativity. Feel the white healing light open your root chakra, releasing tension in your hips and relaxing your thigh muscles. Move down toward your feet, releasing tension in your calves and ankles. Feel this beautiful light activate the chakras in the soles of your feet.

The energy then moves toward the heart of Gaia, connecting and grounding to your earth chakra. Then, visualize this healing light coming up through the ground, surrounding you in light and burning away attachments that no longer serve you. This energy moves through each layer of your aura, cleansing and activating each. The light soon reaches the Merkabah above your crown chakra, completing the circle of light and activating your astral body.

As your physical body stays in healing, your astral body travels to your personal sanctuary, a place between worlds that connects you to your guides and soul. Take a moment to look around your sanctuary and get reacquainted with this space, as you have been here many times. This time, you will notice a fireplace with two doors on each side. You will move toward the door on the left. There you may find an angel or a spirit guide waiting for you. It's okay if there is no one at the door. The door will open when you are ready. Allow yourself to sit with that door in the deep trance-like state until it opens. Once it opens, you will notice a room that seems to have no end and no beginning. It looks as if it is beyond dimension, and it is. It has no dimension and lies in a place beyond time and space.

When granted access to this place, you have arrived at the Akashic records. *Akashic* comes from the Sanskrit word *Akasha*, meaning "ether" or "space." It refers to an ethereal substance or field that is said to permeate the universe and hold the energetic imprints of all thoughts, emotions, experiences, and actions. These records hold the information of everything that ever was. The purpose of accessing the Akashic records is to gain spiritual insight, clarity, healing, and guidance. It is believed that by accessing the records, individuals can gain a deeper understanding of their life's purpose, karmic patterns, relationships, and challenges. We visit when our spirit feels a deep need for clarity of purpose. You will know when the time is right for you because you will have the ability to go deep into a trancelike state. You may want to employ a spiritual practitioner to guide you through the meditative state to the trance state the first time you want to access the records.

Once you step into the records, allow your soul and spirit to guide you. You may be taken to a row of books. If that happens, you will be specifically given your book with your journey in it. Allow the visions to do what they will without interference of thought. I have had experiences where clients see no words in the book, only pictures of lifetimes or purpose. I have had clients who never picked up a book yet went beyond the records to a place they called home. Others had ceremonial experiences where they were granted access to new levels of their human experience. This may take some time and practice to reach; however, once you have walked through the door, you have the key for life.

The Third Eye Activation

The pineal gland is a small endocrine gland located specifically in the epithalamus region. To me, the pineal gland actually looks like an eye. If you take your thumb and tuck it under your fingers, then take a look at your fist from the side, it creates the image of what your pineal gland looks like. The pineal gland is believed to hold the ability to expand awareness when it is fully functioning and healthy.

Science has found that the pineal gland is responsible for the hormone production of melatonin. Melatonin is in charge of your circadian sleep patterns. The pineal gland is signaled by the change in light and dark, so when it's dark out, it is told to produce more melatonin to put the brain to sleep, and consequently when it is light out, it is told to stop the production. One sure way to know if your pineal gland is out of balance is how natural your sleep pattern is. The pineal gland is also believed to help regulate your mood, sexual development, and the immune system. It is important to have a fully working pineal gland for your overall health and mental clarity.

One way to help with the function of the pineal gland is to eat a clean, healthy diet, staying away from chemicals, unnatural caffeine or too much caffeine, and processed foods. A diet that consists of fruits, vegetables, and herbs is a good start to a high-functioning pineal gland. However, it is not the only way. Another way is through energy work. You can have a reiki master do this for you or you can do it yourself. You'll need to have good visualization for this activation. Your practice should be well developed by this point. You can do this laying down or sitting up, whatever is most comfortable for you.

Place your right hand on the back of your head at the top of your neck and your left hand on your forehead. You are going to create a circuit of energy starting in your right hand, going to the pineal gland in the center of your mind, then all the way through your forehead at the "outer" third eye. See this energy then going above your mind to a six-pointed star (the Merkabah) and back down to your right hand, creating a stream of cleansing energy. As the energy streams through your mind, you will then see a closed pine cone. Visualize this pine cone opening like a flower, but as it opens, it releases small beads of light "seeds." This light is activating and cleansing the mind, bringing balance back to that very important hormone. You can do this as often or as little as you like. You want to keep the intention of bringing the pineal gland into balance, not overstimulating it. You will have clear confirmation this is helping when you notice your sleep cycles improving.

Ritual

The third eye rituals that I find most effective are done with shamans. These are about opening yourself up to get clarity and see with certainty the energy around you. There are many to choose from: a pipe ceremony, sweat lodge, ayahuasca, and more. However, since some of these options stem from Indigenous spiritual practices, please also be respectful and only engage in them when invited by a person of those communities. These are to be used sparingly and only when spirit calls you to them.

However, there is one ritual that I use to get my third eye open. I close my eyes and turn toward the sun, but I see everything around me. I absorb the sun into the center of my forehead as often as possible. I do this standing with my feet bare against the earth. I try to stand on natural earth outside when the weather permits, but even if I stand at a window, I stand with my feet bare against the floor. This absorbs the light and connects you to the vibration of the earth at the same time. I think of these moments as connecting me to above and below.

Psychic Center of the Third Eye

Clairvoyance is the ability to gain visual telepathic and psychic information. The third eye is all about sight—internal and external. Mastering the art of energetic sight is an extremely powerful tool. Completing the shadow work for each of the chakras and then clearing and balancing your third eye can have extreme benefits such as creating and maintaining a life full of spiritual alignment and an influx of joy. Here, truly, anything is possible!

Once you have become clear and balanced in the third eye chakra, you may naturally begin to have very clear and vivid dreams. These dreams may be very strange to you and not at all like the normal pattern of dreams you experience. All of this is an indication that your abilities to see things your normal eyes can't are starting to open up. Two of the abilities you can start to develop once this happens are remote viewing and dreamwalking. Both take a lot of practice and come easier after you have fully developed your visualization skills and taken your meditation to the level of a trancelike state.

Remote Viewing

Remote viewing is used to see locations other than the one you are in. You will need a point of reference, something that you can connect to energetically. For remote viewing, you are not taking your energy body (we will get into that more with astral travel in the next chapter); this is simply seeing a place you are not currently at. For example, if someone wants you to locate a lost item of theirs yet you are not in the place they believe they have misplaced it, you can connect to their energy and follow it in your sight back to the lost item. If you want to check on your kids or another loved one, you simply "connect" to their energy and follow the path to where they are.

Depending on how practiced you are at connecting, you may need an object of theirs saturated with their energy in order to tap into it and follow the "scent." It is not really a scent you are following; however, you can think of it like that. You are following an energetic footprint, and once you have arrived at the location, that energetic footprint then combines and interacts with every other energetic footprint around, whether it be a couch, a person, or even what they may be eating. It takes time to decode the different energetic vibrations of objects, but once you have practiced decoding, it comes into focus just as if you are in the room with them.

The first time I did this it was like looking through an old glass Coke bottle: things were a bit distorted, but I could certainly make out what was a couch and what was a person. Just like with anything else, remote viewing gets clearer and clearer the more you practice.

Start by creating the circuit of energy from the third eye (the pineal gland) to the forehead and the Merkabah (or six-pointed star) above your crown chakra. See and feel this energy flow seamlessly and start to expand with light. Once you have created this circuit of energy, the pineal gland and the Merkabah become activated, and you can start to practice remote viewing by focusing on the person, place, or thing you would like to see.

Dreamwalking

Dreamwalking is a bit different in that you are not going to an actual location with your vision; you are joining up with another person when you are both asleep. Dreamwalking is working in the dream world, also different from astral travel. I have found my dreamwalking mostly occurs when I admire someone. My dream consciousness is drawn to people I find curious, and I'm often pulled to their dreams when I have a desire to get to know them better. This is just how my energy has been programmed to travel; however, I can also control the dreamwalking. In these cases when I am making a conscious effort to visit someone in the dream state, I will often get permission or have a conversation in the waking state with the person in order to establish a purpose for the visit. The possibilities of dreamwalking are endless.

Just like with remote viewing, you want to activate your pineal gland and Merkabah, but this time you want to do it specifically as you are falling asleep. During the energy flow, you will think of the person you want to visit. You may even think of the conversation you want to have. You may not have the dreamwalking happen as soon as you fall asleep, but when it occurs later in the night, you will most likely wake up when you return from the person you were visiting. You may want to have a dream journal next to your bed so you can write down key words for your memory. It is truly an exhilarating experience when you call the person the next day and you both experienced the same thing.

Chapter Eight

Crown Chakra, Sahasrara

Located slightly above the top of the head but below the Merka-bah, the energy of the crown deals with knowledge and wisdom. This energy center produces the knowledge beyond the self, where we connect to the collective or universal consciousness. This is the energy center where we receive divine messages.

There are different sources of divine energy. The God source energy will often make you cry, not from sadness actually, quite the opposite: from truth and joy. I like to explain that it feels like wholeness, a complete connection to all things. It is an undeni-able feeling and can completely put everything back into a state of unconditional love.

Then there is the next divine source of energy: the Collective source energy. I find that this is the most channeled energy among light workers. This source energy often takes a combined person-ality of nonbinary characteristics, sometimes called the Ascended Masters but always referred to as "they" or "them."

The next source of divine comes in forms of character traits and strengths and appears when needed most in someone's life. These are known as deities, gods, and saints. Christ embodies the energy of unconditional love; Mary comes when you need to be nurtured and healed. Isis shows you your royal power, and Loki comes to remind us not everything is so serious. Each traditional culture has their own deities, gods, and saints, and each of them embody a specific energy. These divine entities are to be channeled when the specific power they provide is needed. There are many books and rituals used at this level to help you tap into the source energy of the divine you desire.

When working with the crown, we have to learn what filters we have in our ego and the noise of the world that we have focused on. We tend to stay within comfortable parameters, and we need to expand those. Just like with the third eye, the RAS has to be open in order to find the energy source of the Divine, or you will land on the airwaves of humankind and be deceived by the human ego. Many people claim to be tapped into divine source energy, and truthfully it is possible for absolutely everyone to access. No one possesses powers that others cannot. It is simply a matter of development. Of course, some may have stronger natural talents than others, but just as everything else can be learned, so can this.

I have learned in my practice that the ego voice of information comes in at the bottom of the mind. You can almost feel the information coming in low below the pineal gland. The divine source information or divine downloads come in above the mind, where the energy center of the crown sits. With practice, you will eventually be able to physically feel where the knowledge comes into the mind if you open your awareness to it.

I Know

The affirmation "I know" reflects the all-knowing and transcendent qualities of this chakra. It emphasizes the capacity to connect with universal wisdom, experience spiritual awareness, and attain a deep understanding of the interconnectedness of all things. A clear, balanced crown allows you to tap into the universal collective as well as divine consciousness.

I know the wisdom in the energy of all things. I connect and open up to multiple realities and pathways with complete understanding.

Tools and Properties of the Crown for Alignment

Emotional connections: Light body connection to physical body, gateway to dimensions, higher vibrations, higher self, interconnectedness to universal consciousness, heal connection to God, God-self, connection to spiritual family, enlightenment, transcendence, oneness

Physical connections: The brain

Foods: Fasting is recommended for a crown detox and alignment

Activities: Ecstatic dance, Transcendental Meditation

Color: Gold-white, opal, and iridescent—The crown responds to these in high luminosity and balances when exposed to whites.

Element: Divine energy—Sit in sacred space and connect to light.

Tones and notes: B, ee, hew—Listening to music, sounds, and frequencies that have these in them can break up blocks and clear out energy in the crown. Sounds can be a very healing tool for anyone to use. Attend a sound healing class or listen to frequencies on any music app.

Gemstones

Gemstones have many uses for healing and vibrational alignment. They are widely used in holistic practices among many cultures. If you choose to work on one chakra at a time the way this book is laid out, you may want to wear gemstones as jewelry to create a vibrational frequency that aligns to the energy you are moving through. However, you can use them during meditation either on an altar or placed upon the chakra you are working with. You may want to set a routine for this type of meditation or for when you are in the middle of experiencing the emotions. Setting multiple gemstones together around the house in a patterned grid amplifies the energy you are working with and creates movement of this energy. You can do this during the entire cycle of working with this chakra, then change the grid when you move to the next chakra.

Amethyst: This stone enhances spiritual growth, intuition, and awareness. It is used in meditation and spiritual practices to quiet the mind, promote clarity, and deepen one's connection to higher consciousness. Amethyst helps relieve stress, anxiety, and emotional turmoil, promoting a sense of peace, balance, and relaxation. Amethyst enhances spiritual insight and psychic abilities. It helps access higher realms of consciousness and promote spiritual wisdom and guidance.

Clear quartz: This stone enhances the energy of other crystals and objects, making it a valuable tool for manifestation, healing, and spiritual work. It is used to magnify the energy of intentions, affirmations, and visualizations. Clear quartz enhances mental clarity, focus, and concentration. It helps clear mental fog, dispel confusion, and promote a sense of mental and emotional balance. Clear quartz helps open and activate the higher chakras, facilitating a deeper connection to higher realms, spiritual guides, and one's higher self. Clear quartz enhances the power and clarity of intentions, helping to manifest desired outcomes and goals.

Moonstone: This stone enhances psychic abilities, intuition, and emotional intelligence. Moonstone is associated with feminine energy and the divine feminine. It enhances the qualities of compassion, nurturing, and receptivity. Moonstone is often used to connect with and empower the feminine aspect within oneself, promoting self-acceptance, self-care, and emotional healing. Moonstone supports transitions, transformations, and the manifestation of one's intentions. It is often used during times of change or when embarking on new ventures to bring clarity, vision, and positive energy. Moonstone opens the mind to receive intuitive insights, messages, and guidance. Moonstone is often used in meditation, dream work, and other spiritual practices to enhance intuition and deepen spiritual connection.

Selenite: This stone facilitates communication with higher realms, spirit guides, and angels. Selenite has a harmonizing effect on the energy centers (chakras) of the body. It helps remove energy blockages, balances the flow of energy, and promotes overall energetic well-being. Selenite wands are commonly used to sweep the energy field and chakras for clearing and balancing. Selenite is used to calm the mind, clear mental clutter, and promote mental and emotional stability. It can be helpful in meditation, study, and decision-making processes. Selenite creates a protective shield around the aura, preventing the intrusion of negative energies. It is often used for aura cleansing, energy shielding, and maintaining a positive energetic environment.

Celestite: This stone facilitates communication with angels, spirit guides, and higher realms. It opens a direct line of communication, making it easier to receive guidance, messages, and insights from the spiritual realm. Celestite has a gentle and calming energy. It brings peace, tranquility, and a sense of deep relaxation. Celestite balances and aligns the energy centers (chakras) of the body, creating a sense of overall well-being and energetic harmony. Celestite is often used in energy healing and meditation practices to promote inner balance and tranquility.

Oils and Herbs

As with gemstones, oils and herbs can be used in many ways during the healing process. I like to use these specifically during difficult times while working through each energy field. Not only can you experience moments of intense emotion, you may also experience what's called a healing crisis. Sometimes during a healing crisis it can feel like you have flu-like symptoms. This is actually the toxins leaving the body. You can experience this after a reiki session or sometimes after a yoga sequence. There are other times you may experience a healing crisis, and in these instances, I find it useful to use the oils and herbs. This is also a good time to drink the tea blends.

Frankincense: This plant creates a sacred and serene atmosphere, promoting a sense of tranquility and heightened awareness. Frankincense helps quiet the mind, uplift the spirit, and facilitate a deeper connection to the Divine. It creates a shield of spiritual protection, warding off negative energies and entities. Frankincense is often used in rituals and incense blends for energetic protection and to create a sense of sacred space. Frankincense supports personal growth, expands consciousness, and deepens spiritual understanding. Frankincense is often used in rituals and practices aimed at spiritual transformation and self-realization.

Myrrh: This plant strengthens the connection with ancestral spirits and brings their guidance and blessings. Myrrh is used in rituals and ceremonies to commemorate and honor ancestors. Myrrh is used to create a sacred and introspective atmosphere, promoting a sense of calmness and inner reflection. Myrrh helps quiet the mind, center the spirit, and facilitate a deeper connection to higher realms.

Sage: This herb promotes clarity of thought. It is used to quiet the mind, clear mental clutter, and enhance spiritual insights. Sage can be used in meditation and divination practices to deepen intuition and access higher wisdom. Be mindful that sage is overharvested. Try to get sage from Indigenous communities.

Lotus: The lotus is seen as a symbol of spiritual enlightenment and the journey to awakening. It represents the transformation from darkness to light, ignorance to wisdom. The lotus flower inspires spiritual growth, inner clarity, and the realization of one's true nature. The lotus is considered a sacred and divine flower in many spiritual traditions. It represents the divine presence and purity. The lotus is associated with spiritual figures and deities, symbolizing their enlightened nature and connection to the Divine. The lotus facilitates a connection to the higher self or soul. It is associated with the opening of the spiritual heart and the realization of one's true nature. The lotus flower is often used as a symbol to deepen the connection to one's inner wisdom and higher consciousness.

Juniper: This plant enhances spiritual connection and intuition. It opens channels of communication with higher realms, guides, and spiritual beings. Juniper can be used in meditation, prayer, or divination practices to deepen spiritual experiences and insights. It creates uplifting and positive energies and promotes a sense of joy, optimism, and vitality. Juniper can be used to shift stagnant or negative energies, inviting positive vibrations and creating a more vibrant atmosphere.

Shadow Work

The following practice is the flow I like to use when doing my own shadow work. There is no wrong way. Find what works for you and move at your own pace.

1. Where are your physical issues? If you have stomach issues, maybe start with the solar plexus. If you are not sure about what is physically out of alignment, I would simply start with the root and move up from there.

2. Once you decide which chakra you are going to start focusing on, put your energy and thoughts toward that chakra at night. Even before knowing what may come up, simply put your hands on that energy center as you fall asleep. You can send healing light visually to that chakra and say out loud or to yourself "I am ready to release any stuck and unhealed energy. I am ready to see what has been hiding in the shadows." Then be

open to what happens next. Your days to follow will bring up issues you have been avoiding.

3. Set time aside weekly for processing the emotions, emotional reactions, triggers, and social interactions that are coming up. You may even want to do this daily before you go to bed. Start journaling the questions you are asking and answering for yourself.

4. Finally, decide which of the provided tools you will use and create a routine for each. Slowly integrate changes into your routine. Do not try to do everything all at once. In order to create sustainable lifestyle changes, you should start with one at a time. After you feel comfortable with steps two and three, maybe add drinking herbal teas or yoga once a week.

Questions for Crown Chakra Shadow Work

Be open to looking at what influences your thoughts and the way your mind processes information. What are you feeding your mind? What words, beliefs, and conversations are you engaging in? How do you approach or explore the quest for a higher understanding of all things? Ask yourself, how can you go beyond what you know now? It's not about sitting in constant study, reading books, or watching documentaries. It's about being open to the information, and the information will find you. You may accidentally find that one documentary that takes you on a six-month journey of new information and experiences. This happened to me when I accidentally stumbled upon *Fantastic Fungi*. Learning about mycelium and how it communicates actually created a connection for me in my brain. This system of life showed me exactly how I and other psychics theoretically connect to others' energy pathways.

When you tell yourself you want to understand deeply, your RAS will be open to the information that is already around you, and you will start to experience new information. Ask yourself, are you satisfied with the answers you already have? The answer here should be no. If you are, then you have attached to a destination and you are no longer willing to move forward. Always keep going with new experiences of living, learning, and healing.

During my shadow work in the crown, I had to understand what it meant for me to have an ADHD brain, and I learned how to work with it. For me it was never nurtured as a label to hinder my experience. Learning about the way this type of mind functions was extremely helpful and not at all a burden but instead offered more freedom. Sometimes a diagnosis can help create self-awareness.

In that seeking and understanding, I learned how to decipher the different wavelengths in my mind. I could start to identify what was the ego and what was the spirit. This work allowed me to listen to my brain in more depth and filter out other people's egos. I discovered my true nature of joy and happiness and let go of the voices that resonated fear, doubt, indecision, uncertainty, and the thought of "should." In doing the shadow work with each of the chakras, it was easier to identify and let go of voices that created chaos to my peace. I became highly aware of where and how my perceptions were formed and what was truly my voice. I became aware that experiencing emotions did not have to disrupt my natural state of happiness. I began to see and truly understand that we cannot create from a state of attachment. Attachment will recycle the past, and we will continue to get what we know instead of creating new.

Letter for the Crown Chakra Shadow Work

At times we get blocked by the limitations of our own information, which creates a narrowed perspective of an event or circumstance in our lives. While writing the crown chakra letter, think of your mind expanding, gaining new insight, and seeing all sides of the event or circumstance. You'll be amazed at the information that will show up for you.

> *Show me deeper understandings and a full view of all things. Give me clarity and wisdom.*

Letters to Write Daily When Healing the Crown Chakra

This letter can be short, brief, and daily, more like a morning ritual than a letter. However, we will still put it in letter form every morning.

> *Dear Universe, the Divine, the Ancient Ones, I open up to deep understanding and clarity. I know more than I realize, and I open my mind for deeper wisdom in all things. I know there are divine things present in every moment all around me, and I am open to receive. I willingly go into new experiences with an open mind and soul.*

Affirmations for Crown Chakra Energy Work

I know new information daily!
I know new energies and voices!
I know new experiences!
I know all things are connected!

Recipes for Crown Chakra Energy Work

For each tea blend, I use loose-leaf herbs and tea leaves and make the blends in 20-ounce Mason jars. I use about ⅓ of a cup for each ingredient. I gently roll the Mason jar to mix the ingredients together without breaking up the herbs into dust.

When I'm ready to brew the tea, I heat up water in a teapot and scoop a tablespoon of the blend into a reusable tea bag. I then add my tea bag plus other ingredients such as honey or lemon (to taste) to a mug before the water is done. When the water is hot, I add it to the mug slowly.

To activate the tea with the incantation, I do a few things: First, I will write the incantation onto a sticky note and put it on the pot as it heats the water. As I pour the water slowly, I will read the incantation out loud. I stop the pour with enough room at the top of my mug so that the next part does not cause the water to spill out. Once the water is a little cooled down, I will place my right hand over the top of the mug and grasp it (not by its handle but by the rim) so that the energy from my hand is also infused into the water. Once I have a firm grip, I will pick it up and swirl the mug and tea clockwise three times while saying the incantation. I will also repeat this on my left side three times but counterclockwise. Then I will go back to my right hand and repeat the swirl but counterclockwise then left hand clockwise.

Your tea is now fully infused with the energy you intend, and once it is cooled down enough to drink, enjoy.

Divini-Tea and Incantation

- Lavender, sage, jasmine, green tea, full moon water

"My mind awakened. My soul connected. Source light energy, I receive."

Clari-Tea and Incantation

• Chamomile, dandelion, lilac, full moon water

"I know a higher me. I know clearly. I know new pathways, open to all."

Movement and Yoga Sequence for the Crown

Balancing and opening your crown chakra can be done every day. Whether you simply meditate or do a movement sequence, there is always something you can do to know life more clearly.

1. **Sun Salutation (Surya Namaskar):**
   • Start in mountain pose (tadasana) at the top of your mat, feet hip-width apart, and palms together at your heart center.
   • Inhale, raise your arms overhead, and arch your back slightly, coming into upward salute (urdhva hastasana).
   • Exhale, hinge forward at your hips, and bring your hands to the mat beside your feet, coming into forward fold (uttanasana).
   • Inhale, lift halfway up, lengthening your spine and bringing your hands to your shins or fingertips to the floor, coming into halfway lift (ardha uttanasana).
   • Exhale, step or jump your feet back into a high plank position (utthita chaturanga dandasana).
   • Lower your body down slowly, elbows tucked in, into low plank (chaturanga dandasana).
   • Inhale, roll over your toes, lift your chest, and come into upward-facing dog (urdhva mukha svanasana),

keeping your thighs off the mat and shoulders away from your ears.

- Exhale, tuck your toes, lift your hips up and back, and come into downward-facing dog (adho mukha svanasana). Hold for a few breaths.
- Exhale, fold forward (uttanasana).
- Inhale, sweep your arms wide, and come up to standing, reaching your arms overhead, returning to upward salute (urdhva hastasana).
- Exhale, bring your hands back to your heart center, returning to mountain pose (tadasana).
- Repeat the above steps for a few rounds, synchronizing your breath with each movement.

2. **Cat-Cow Pose (Marjaryasana-Bitilasana):**
- Start on your hands and knees, with your hands under your shoulders and knees under your hips.
- Inhale, arch your back, lift your chest, and drop your belly toward the mat, coming into cow pose.
- Exhale, round your spine, tuck your chin toward your chest, and draw your belly button toward your spine, coming into cat pose.
- Continue flowing between cat and cow, syncing your breath with each movement.
- Repeat for several rounds, allowing your spine to move fluidly.

3. **Tree Pose (Vrikshasana):**
- Start in mountain pose, grounding through your left foot.

- Shift your weight onto your left foot and lift your right foot off the ground, placing the sole of your right foot against the inside of your left calf or thigh, avoiding placing it directly on your knee.
- Find your balance, keeping your gaze steady on a focal point.
- Bring your hands together at your heart center or reach your arms overhead, maintaining a tall and stable posture.
- Hold the pose for several breaths, then repeat on the opposite side.

4. **Backbend (Chakrasana):**
    - Start by lying on your belly with your legs extended and feet hip-width apart.
    - Place your hands on the mat next to your shoulders, fingers pointing toward your body.
    - Inhale, press into your hands, and lift your chest off the mat, keeping your lower body grounded.
    - Draw your shoulder blades toward each other, opening your chest and gently arching your back.
    - Take a few deep breaths in this position, feeling the stretch in your front body.
    - Exhale, slowly lower your chest back down to the mat.
    - Repeat the backbend a few times, allowing your breath to guide your movement.

5. **Rabbit Pose (Sasangasana):**

   - Start in a kneeling position, with your hips lifted from your heels.

   - Place your hands on the back of your heels, fingers pointing toward your toes.

   - Inhale, tuck your chin toward your chest, and round your spine, rolling your forehead toward your knees.

   - Hold the pose for a few breaths, feeling the stretch along your spine and the back of your body.

   - Exhale, slowly release the pose, returning to a neutral position.

6. **Corpse Pose (Savasana):**

   - Lie down on your back, extending your legs and allowing your feet to fall out to the sides.

   - Relax your arms alongside your body, palms facing up.

   - Close your eyes and take slow, deep breaths, allowing your body to settle into the mat.

   - Bring your awareness to each part of your body, consciously releasing tension and inviting relaxation.

   - Stay in savasana for a few minutes, allowing yourself to rest and rejuvenate.

Meditations

You are about to revisit each chakra in the next meditation. Chakra Beach was a place I was introduced to as a young child, and through the years it has always served as a place that offers pure energy healing. It wasn't until later years that messages started to appear during this meditation. Mostly this meditation is about putting you back into a state of whole, balanced vibration.

Chakra Beach

Get yourself in a comfortable position sitting or lying down. Start with the centering and grounding meditation, filling your mind, body, and energy system with the white light as it works its way down your body, connecting and grounding you, then surrounding you and cleansing your energy aura finally connecting to the six-pointed star, Merkabah above the crown. Once the flow of energy is completed and you are surrounded in the light energy, you should be able to begin to flow into a trancelike state at this point.

You will see your spirit body standing upon a beautiful beach of white sands and turquoise water. Your spirit body will be pulled to walk down the beach. As you walk, you will notice a set of red rocks. These red rocks represent your root chakra. The image of the rocks will appear in a form that mirrors what is going on with your chakra energy. You will want to quiet your mind even more than you have practiced in the past in order to allow the Divine to take over. That way, you may see what work might be needed in the root. You will be divinely guided to assist in creating a healing journey for the root. You may be asked to add rocks, subtract rocks, or even organize them differently. You will know what is needed once you have arrived at these gems.

Once you have been guided with the red gemstones, you will proceed down the beach even further until you come upon the orange gemstones. You will continue down this journey, repeating the process of observing each energy center. You will work your way through the sacral (orange), solar plexus (yellow), heart (pink/green), throat (blue), third eye (violet/purple), and crown (white-gold). Once you have reached the crown chakra and completed the journey down the beach, you will sit within your own energy body (on the beach) looking out into the clear turquoise water.

What appears on the water next will be of divine wisdom. I have witnessed clients being guided to walk upon the water, where they are greeted by ancestors and divine beings.

You will be guided out of the experience by the Divine, and you will remember things out of order or even randomly through-out the rest of the day. Each part of this experience holds wisdom and may only be remembered at needed times. Set yourself up with a way to record the experience once you return. Give your-self plenty of space and time to do this one.

Crown Chakra Activation

By the time you get here, you have done so much work. Now it's just a matter of understanding, really. Your meditation practice in combination with your shadow work and yoga have probably already activated your crown chakra and Merkabah. You have a brief understanding of how the energy connects; just as mycelium communicates in the earth below us, we also have the capacity to communicate through networks not seen by the eyes. However, there is one thing I haven't explained to you yet: light language.

Honestly, I have to laugh and find joy in this because, believe it or not, even though I am a writer, I am not good at language, and now I have to find and interpret something that is based in light. I had an experience with a friend who was channeling, and out of frustration and without thought, he proclaimed, "English is hard." Even though we are both English-speaking natives, I knew exactly what he meant while he was in that channeling trance, and we both laughed. The Divine doesn't speak English, Spanish, Italian, or any other language found here on earth, not even Sanskrit. The Divine speaks in light.

How does something speak in light? Well, that is hard to translate in and of itself. It is a "knowing," a feeling, a vibration. That is why we use so many different tools. It is not the tarot, the oracle, the runes, that do the talking; it is the Divine. We just need the interpretations, translations. Each psychic medium has their own set of "tools" or images that mean something to them when they listen to the light language. It is our way of creating the translation for each person we are working with. My language code, ironically, is pop culture references. I say *ironically* because I don't watch TV, but somehow, the spirits always know what to reference in pop culture, and I wind up talking about a show I've never even seen in order to translate the message. I find it quite funny.

This is the work for you, the activation. You have to lean into the light language by simply trusting the random, seemingly silly, symbols the spirits present as you first start. Then you will create your own form of translation. The more tools you explore, the more you will find what works for you and the more comfortable you will become with the language of light. It is not something anyone can create a manuscript for. It is and always will be the way you connect to source energy and the multiple pathways of energy. You will find others who translate light language in a similar fashion to you, but you will still have a unique code that has been created through your experiences and the connections you tap into.

Ritual

The crown is all about divine wisdom, and the best practice I have come across in my life to open up this channel is reading. Read as much as you can. Read about things that you have no experience in. Read both sides of the story and keep reading. You can absolutely make this a ritual. Sunday might be a holy or family day for you. For me, Sunday is the day to read and expand my library of information.

While reading, I often make notes on each page. No matter what type of book I am reading, I find that information gets channeled in with every sentence. This is information that is not written in the text on the page, so I find that writing as I go keeps that channel clear and open, which creates a continuous flow.

You can set your intention before beginning the book and keep a set of pens and pencils dedicated just for this. I always set the intention of learning or studying when I pick up a book. For me, this ritual is professional and personal development.

Psychic Center of the Crown

When the crown chakra is clear and ready to move into the next level of operation, you will find things just start to make sense. You will start to make connections to information you had never made before. Your *aha* moments will happen more often and will begin to transcend your own life. You will start to see the bigger picture with almost everything in life, and your worries about the small stuff will no longer exist. This is when the ability of claircognizance has become activated.

Claircognizance

Claircognizance is clear knowing, intuitive inner knowing, and divine downloads. It is an incredible feeling to know with certainty the things that are streaming through your mind. When you are being guided to share information through claircognizance—things you've never said or even thought before—it is a brilliant exchange of energy for you and whoever you are sharing it with. These moments of clarity can come at any time and may also occur in great detail during any meditation technique you are practicing.

Astral Travel

I wanted to save astral travel for the end because you really need a lot of practice with meditation and activating your energy center in order to open this ability. You also need to be pretty clear in terms of shadow work here. That doesn't mean you need to be a completely healed and transcended human; you just need to have awareness of the ongoing work you need to do. You need to be willing to do that ongoing work. It is my belief that we are human as long as we have a body. When we leave this body, we can then claim to be more than that. This is an advanced technique and most likely will not be achieved until well into your journey. You will want to do this while in a very safe, undisturbed space. Someone who does not know what you are doing may try to "wake" you or disturb your process.

Astral travel is going to be the same process you did with the third eye. You are going to create the circuit of energy from the base of your mind (your pineal gland), forehead, then Merkabah. Once that circuit is created, instead of seeing the pineal gland open and expand like you did in the third eye exercise, you will see and feel the Merkabah descend down around your energy and physical body. The energy body will connect to the Merkabah, leaving the physical body in a deep trancelike state.

When in the astral or light body and lucid, you will be able to see the same things you would see while in the physical body; however, you will also be able to see things that are present that the physical eyes cannot see. If you do this at nighttime, the world will appear as if it is light out. It will still be very bright, and you will be able to see clearly.

There are many energies you could see while walking in the astral. You can see sleeping friends or even strangers. You will be able to see their light bodies also traveling, even if they are not aware of their travels. You can also have friends that are awake and engaging in the waking life; you can be in the kitchen with them or at the party. Your sleeping friends and awake friends may see you. You may actually hear them say your name as if you just "crossed their mind." They may not have awareness of your actual light body presence.

You can also see divine symbols at work, sacred geometry, and really anything with an energy imprint. You can also focus your travel and go to a specific destination, like your home state if you moved away of somewhere you are drawn to. However, you may want to allow the energy to take you where it organically wants to go. Those have been the most exciting, beneficial journeys I have had.

Astral travel has limitless possibilities that I am still discovering. You are capable of discovering more of these on your own. Once you have gotten to this point in the book, you have all the tools you need to create magic in your life. Practice every day! Learn every day! Release the experience every day! Create a life full of abundance worthy of calling a feast!

Conclusion
It's All Energy

Whether you use crystals, herbs, music, meditation, rituals, or movement to assist in the energy work, remember, all you have to do is connect to that energy in order to work with it. If you are clearing the energy, reading the energy, healing the energy, or empowering it, it's about connecting and letting it flow. This journey should take you through many layers of your own energy, all leading to the real you. It is a spiral, and you will revisit each energy center many times as you ascend through your healing and higher levels of vibration. Enjoy the journey and keep coming back.

I would like to leave you with one last event that made significant changes in my life. I know without this dark moment I would not be as happy as I am today. As you move through your life, remember there can be light in any event when you are ready to move through it.

In 2019, I was at my lowest and couldn't possibly get lower. I had taken a handful of pills and had written my letters of goodbye. I was genuinely ready to exit; however, that didn't happen. I was found and went to the hospital and started the detox process. It was the most painful two weeks of my life. Physical pain was greater than the emotional pain. However, I heard two very powerful things that changed my life forever. The first was specific to my life, and that was, "The pain won't die with your body. It will infect the hearts of your children and grow in them like cancer, slowly killing them." That was the first thing that quickly and abruptly changed my baseline, and I knew I had to change, heal, and fight for happiness.

The second thing I heard—and the most profound, with the biggest ripple effect that continues to affect my everyday life— was, "Nothing is real." This was not a simple one-liner but a conversation I like to say I had with God. After I heard "Nothing is real," I began to ask questions that were, in turn, all answered. I asked things like, "What about my knee? Is my knee real?" And I answered, "No." I went through all the body parts and family members before I got to the more philosophical questions like love: "Is love real?" "No." Each time I asked, the answer never faltered; it was always no. At the time, if I'm being honest, it was terrifying; however, the aftermath of what I truly believe was a five-hour conversation has been extremely liberating. I can look at any situation, any circumstance, as nothing more than energy. Nothing truly exists except within the perception of our mind, which in turn means anything is possible and magic is real!

Recommended Reading

Anatomy of Yoga: An Instructor's Inside Guide to Improving Your Poses by Abigail Ellsworth (Richmond Hill, Ontario: Firefly Books, 2010).

Atlas of the Heart: Mapping Meaningful Connection and the Language of Human Experience by Brené Brown (New York: Random House, 2021).

The Body Keeps the Score: Brain, Mind, and Body in the Healing of Trauma by Bessel van der Kolk (New York: Viking, 2014).

The Heart of Yoga: Developing a Personal Practice, revised edition by T. K. V. Desikachar (Rochester, VT: Inner Traditions International, 1999).

The Language of Letting Go: Daily Meditations for Codependents by Melody Beattie (Center City, MN: Hazelden Publishing, 1990).

Reality Unveiled: The Hidden Keys of Existence that Will Transform Your Life (And the World) by Ziad Masri (Awakened Media LLC, 2017).

Wheels of Life: A User's Guide to the Chakra System by Anodea Judith, 2nd ed., revised and expanded (St. Paul, MN: Llewellyn Publications, 1999).

The Yoga Sutras of Patanjali translation and commentary by Sri
    Swami Satchidananda (Yogaville, VA: Integral Yoga Publica-
    tions, 1990).

Bibliography

Desikachar, T. K. V. *The Heart of Yoga: Developing a Personal Practice*. Rochester, VT: Inner Traditions International, 1995.

Rizzolatti, Giacomo, and Laila Craighero. "The Mirror-Neuron System." *Annual Review of Neuroscience* 27 (2004): 169–92. https://doi.org/10.1146/annurev.neuro.27.070203.144230.

Stiles, Mukunda, interpreter. *Yoga Sutras of Patanjali*. Boston, MA: Weiser Books, 2002.

To Write to the Author

If you wish to contact the author or would like more information about this book, please write to the author in care of Llewellyn Worldwide Ltd. and we will forward your request. Both the author and publisher appreciate hearing from you and learning of your enjoyment of this book and how it has helped you. Llewellyn Worldwide Ltd. cannot guarantee that every letter written to the author can be answered, but all will be forwarded. Please write to:

Stefani Michelle
℅ Llewellyn Worldwide
2143 Wooddale Drive
Woodbury, MN 55125-2989

Please enclose a self-addressed stamped envelope for reply,
or $1.00 to cover costs. If outside the U.S.A., enclose
an international postal reply coupon.

Many of Llewellyn's authors have websites with additional information and resources. For more information, please visit our website at http://www.llewellyn.com.